THE TRUTH OF CATHOLICISM

D0302104

ALSO BY GEORGE WEIGEL

Tranquillitas Ordinis: *The Present Failure and Future Promise of American Catholic Thought on War and Peace*

Catholicism and the Renewal of American Democracy

American Interests, American Purpose: Moral Reasoning and U.S. Foreign Policy

Freedom and Its Discontents: Catholicism Confronts Modernity

Just War and the Gulf War [with James Turner Johnson]

The Final Revolution: The Resistance Church and the Collapse of Communism

Idealism Without Illusions: U.S. Foreign Policy in the 1990s

Soul of the World: Notes on the Future of Public Catholicism

Witness to Hope: The Biography of Pope John Paul II

What does being a Catholic mean? Is there a distinctively Catholic way of seeing things? What does the Catholic Church teach about the human condition—about our lives, our loves, and our destiny? In *The Truth of Catholicism*, best-selling author George Weigel explores these perennial questions through the prism of ten contemporary controversies.

The Catholic Church may be the most controversial institution in the world. Some find its teachings inexplicable, puzzling, even cruel. George Weigel suggests that we look at Catholicism and its controversies from "inside" the convictions that make those controversies not only possible, but necessary. The truths of Catholicism then come into clearer focus as affirmations and celebrations of human life and human love, even as they challenge us to imagine a daring future for humanity and for ourselves.

Is Jesus uniquely the savior of the world? Does belief in God limit our freedom? What are we doing when we pray? Is the moral life about rules or about happiness? Doesn't suffering contradict the biblical claim that God is good? How does the Catholic Church think about other Christians and about other great world religions? Are Catholics safe for democracy? What will become of us? In an engaging, accessible style, George Weigel leads us through these and other questions into the truth of Catholicism: the truth about a God passionately in love with his creation, the truth about a love that creates a vast, liberating terrain on which to live a fully human life.

GEORGE WEIGEL is the author of the international bestseller *Witness to Hope: The Biography of Pope John Paul II*. A Roman Catholic theologian and senior fellow of the Ethics and Public Policy Center, he is one of the world's preeminent commentators on the Catholic Church.

THE TRUTH OF CATHOLICISM

TEN CONTROVERSIES EXPLORED

GEORGE WEIGEL

GRACEWING

First published in 2001 by HarperCollins, New York
This edition published in 2002 by

Gracewing
2 Southern Avenue
Leominster
Herefordshire HR6 0QF

Published by arrangement with HarperCollins Publishers, Inc., New York, New York, USA. All rights reserved. No part of this publication may be reproduced, stored in a retrieval system, or transmitted in any form, or by any means, electronic, mechanical, photocopying, recording, or otherwise, without the written permission of the publisher.

© George Weigel 2001

The right of George Weigel to be identified as the author of this work has been asserted in accordance with the Copyright, Designs and Patents Act 1988.

Jacket design by Margaret Mirabile. Jacket photograph, *The fan vaulting of the retrochoir by Master John Wastell, Peterborough*, from Library, Getty Research Institute, Los Angeles:
Wim Swaan Photograph Collection (96.P.21)

ISBN 0 85244 572 5

Printed in England by
Antony Rowe Ltd
Chippenham
Wiltshire SN14 6LH

For
the Faculty, Staff, and Students of the
Pontifical North American College in Rome,
1995–2000

Contents

An Invitation to Come Inside

The great English novelist Evelyn Waugh once described his Catholic life as "an endless delighted tour of discovery in the huge territory of which I was made free." Like many other converts, Waugh was eager to share that adventure with others, and his correspondence is full of letters explaining Catholicism to his friends. At the same time, Waugh's experience had taught him that it was very difficult to "know what the Church is like from outside." To all the curious, whether attracted or disturbed by Catholicism's teaching and the Catholic way of life, Evelyn Waugh offered a simple invitation: "Come inside." Have a look at the Catholic Church from inside the convictions that make Catholicism what it is. Walk around in it. See how it feels. Then decide what you think about it.[1]

At the beginning of the third millennium of Christian history, that simple suggestion to "come inside" can be as inviting as it was when Evelyn Waugh first issued it a half century ago. Or when, nineteen and a half centuries ago, St. Paul proposed much the same thing to those Athenians who worshiped the "unknown god" (*Acts* 17.16–34).[2]

The Catholic Church is, arguably, the most controversial institution on the planet; it is certainly the world's most controversial religious institution. Whether the question is the uniqueness of Christ, the meaning of freedom, the dignity of human life from conception until natural death, or the use and abuse of sex, the Catholic Church often finds itself a Church of contradiction, in opposition to what seems to be the common wisdom of our times. Because of that, the Church is sometimes an object of hatred and scorn, especially for those who think that the Church's teachings dehumanize or marginalize them.

Even those who concede that religious faith can be "good for" some people often imagine faith as another lifestyle choice, of no greater consequence than choosing one's car, pet, or favorite restaurant. In these circumstances, the Catholic Church's steady insistence that faith involves truths, that those truths involve obligations, and that those obligations demand certain choices can be intimidating, even repellent. Viewed from outside, the Catholic Church can seem narrow-minded, crabby, and pinched—the heckling preacher of an endless string of prohibitions.

Which is very strange, because Catholicism is about affirmation: the affirmation of humanity, and of every individual human life, by a God passionately in love with his creation. So in love, in fact, that he sent his Son into the world for the world's salvation. But what Catholicism *is* is often not apparent from outside.

This small book explores ten of the controversies provoked by Catholicism today, from inside the convictions that make those controversies necessary. It is intended for Catholics who are anxious, curious, or unsure about what their Church really teaches and why, and Catholics who want to share their beliefs with friends and family, especially the young. It is equally intended for the many people who find it difficult to reconcile their admiration for certain Catholics—Mother Teresa of Calcutta, Pope John Paul II, their next-door neighbor, or their coworker—with what seem incomprehensible, even cruel, doctrines. By coming inside and seeing how the Catholic vision of the human condition and the human prospect fit together, both the curious and the discontented will, it is hoped, be able to see affirmation and celebration of the human project in Catholicism, not condemnation and mindless prohibition.

The book should be read "inside out" in another way. Please resist the temptation to jump first to the sexy issues, literally and figuratively. The Catholic Church is far less obsessed with sex than the media is with Catholic teachings about sex. Prior to World Youth Day in Paris in 1997, the press agency of the French bishops commissioned a study that determined that something like 3 percent of Pope John Paul II's public statements during the previous nineteen years had had something to do with issues of sexual morality. Yet, as the bishops' spokesmen pointed out, to read a lot of the world press you'd have thought that sex was all the Pope ever talked, or worried, about. The Catholic Church takes sex seriously, far more seriously than the editors of either *Playboy* or *Cosmopolitan*. If we want to understand the *what* and the *why* of the Catholic sexual ethic, though, we have to engage it within the broader context of Catholic teaching about who we are, about what reality is, and ultimately about who God is. The Bible doesn't begin with the Ten Commandments. It begins with stories of the world's creation and with God's affirmation that the world he created is good.

So, please—come inside. No one will force you to stay. But once inside, you may find that what seemed cramped and confining is in fact, as Evelyn Waugh suggested, a huge and liberating terrain on which to live a fully human life—and to prepare for a destiny beyond mundane imagining.

1

Is Jesus the Only Savior?

Christ and the Conquest of Our Fears

In September 2000, the Vatican's Congregation for the Doctrine of the Faith, often described as "the successor to the Inquisition," caused a global uproar by issuing a doctrinal declaration, *Dominus Iesus* [The Lord Jesus], which vigorously reasserted the classic Christian teaching that Jesus Christ is uniquely the savior of the world, for everyone everywhere. The ensuing controversy had some sharp edges.

One American newspaper displayed a photo of Pope John Paul II, arms outstretched, with the caption "We're Number One!" More soberly but no less inaccurately, another major paper headlined the story "Vatican Declares Catholicism Sole Path to Salvation." According to most of the stories and commentaries that followed, the declaration had done serious and perhaps even fatal damage to thirty years of ecumenical and interreligious dialogue. As the common interpretation of

Dominus Iesus had it, the Catholic Church was teaching that Catholics had a singular claim on salvation and that non-Catholic Christians were second-class Christians. As for Jews, Muslims, Buddhists, Hindus, and nonbelievers, well . . .

None of this was, or is, true, but that is not an easy case to make in a climate in which a lot of people are not sure that anything is "true." ("It depends on what the meaning of the word 'is' is," as a prominent public figure once said.) In fact, *Dominus Iesus* taught nothing new, substantively. One distinguished Catholic commentator put the case for the defense succinctly: the declaration reiterated "the Church's faith that Jesus is, as he said of himself, the way, the truth, and the life. He is not one way among other ways or one truth among other truths."[1] That faith in Jesus Christ leads to other convictions, also affirmed once again in *Dominus Iesus*. Because there is one God, who definitively revealed himself in his Son, Jesus Christ, there is one salvation history, centered on Christ. God gives everyone the grace necessary to be saved, including those who have never heard of Jesus Christ. Yet everyone who is saved is saved because of what God did for the world and for humanity in Jesus Christ.

Before, during, and after the *Dominus Iesus* controversy, one had to wonder just what else the Catholic Church was supposed to say about itself: that it was another brand-name product in the supermarket of "spirituality"? Yet in a culture that rates tolerance the highest virtue and imagines that tolerance means indifference to questions about the truth of things, the unambiguous claim that this is *the* truth, and that all other truths incline toward this truth as iron shavings incline to a magnet, is not just controversial. It's an outrage.

The frankness of *Dominus Iesus* may be applauded one day, when passions have cooled a bit. At a moment in history when ecumenical and interreligious dialogue threatened to dissolve into dull and uninteresting forms of political correctness of the "I'm OK, you're OK" variety, the chief doctrinal agency of the Catholic Church reminded the Church and the world that Christianity stands or falls on the answer the Church and its people give to a single question. The question has been unavoidable for almost two thousand years. It is the question Jesus himself posed to his disciples on the road to Caesarea Philippi: "Who do you say that I am?" (*Matthew* 16.15).

Who does the Catholic Church say that Jesus is?

The Two Things Jesus Reveals

The Second Vatican Council, which met between 1962 and 1965, was the most important event in world Catholicism since the sixteenth-century Reformation. Among many other things, the Council tried to open a two-way dialogue between the Church and contemporary culture. In a lengthy document called the *Pastoral Constitution on the Church in the Modern World,* the bishops of the Catholic Church wrote that Jesus, the Son of God come into the world, reveals the face of God and his love, and the full meaning of our humanity.[2] The two go together. To know the Son is to know the Father; to know the Father and the Son is to know, ultimately, who we are.

Who is the God whom Jesus reveals? He is a God who is

linked to us not simply as the source of creation, distant and detached, but as "Father," intimately present to us through the gift of his Son.[3] He is a God who comes in search of us, a God who is not a stranger to history but a participant in the human drama. He is a "God who has gone before us and leads us on, who himself set out on man's path, a God who does not look down on us from on high, but who became our traveling companion."[4]

God's fidelity, powerfully conveyed in Jesus' parable of the prodigal son (*Luke* 15.11–32), is not remote and austere but passionately affectionate. To believe in this God, the Father of Jesus Christ, is to believe that order and reason, rather than chaos and indifference, are at the root of things. To know this Father, through Jesus Christ, means to know "that love is present in the world, and that this love is more powerful than any kind of evil."[5]

We "cannot live without love," Pope John Paul II writes. We cannot understand ourselves, we cannot make sense of life, unless love comes to us and we "participate intimately" in it.[6] We sense our profound need for love instinctively. The God whom Jesus reveals is the guarantor that this intuition is one of the great truths of the human condition, not a psychological illusion.

And what is the humanity that Jesus reveals? Who are we? We are not congealed stardust, an accidental by-product of cosmic chemistry. We are not just some*thing,* we are *someone.*[7] Moreover, we are "someones" going *somewhere.* As human beings possessed of an innate, God-given dignity, we have a divine destiny, revealed and made possible by Jesus Christ. That destiny was defined boldly by the fourth-century theologian St. Athanasius, who claimed that "the Son of God became man so that we might become God."[8] Nine centuries later, St. Thomas Aquinas, the master of philosophically logical theology, agreed: "The only-begotten Son of God . . . assumed our nature, so that he, made man, might make men gods."[9]

Moreover, the Church teaches that this divine destiny is not something promised for an indeterminate future; it is something we can experience now, in a personal relationship with Jesus Christ. To live in communion with Jesus Christ now, through the Church that continues his presence in the world and in history, is far more than a matter of joining a voluntary organization dedicated to good causes. It is to live in an anticipatory way in the Kingdom of God. In this sense, Christians are the people who already know how the world's story is going to turn out and who live that dramatic, life-affirming destiny here and now.

These bold affirmations of humanity's divine origins and future are not peripheral to the Catholic view of things. They are bedrock truths of faith. They are also Catholicism's answer to a perennial criticism: that faith in Jesus Christ robs us of maturity, condemns us to endless adolescent dependence, and promotes a romantically unrealistic view of the world. "You have made us for yourself," St. Augustine wrote of God's intentions toward us, "and our hearts are restless until they rest in you."[10] That restlessness is a summons to deepen, not avoid, our humanity. That is what meeting Jesus Christ means.

The Catholic view of human dignity and destiny, as revealed in Jesus Christ, is profoundly countercultural in one important respect. For more than two hundred years the idea that human fulfillment comes through self-assertion has been widespread in Western societies. The Catholic claim, which is true to the teaching of Jesus, is precisely the opposite. The Church's claim is that we reach our fulfillment as human beings not by asserting ourselves, but by giving ourselves—by making ourselves into the gift to others that life itself is to us.

That none of us is the cause of our own existence is no mere accident of biology; it is an empirical fact that, viewed through the lens of faith, reveals a profound truth about the human condition. Self-assertion, on the Catholic view of things, is the "original sin," the perennial human temptation that beset Adam and Eve at the very beginning of the human story.[11] Self-giving, according to the Second Vatican Council, is the royal road to human happiness: we discover our true selves in a "sincere giving" of ourselves.[12] In a culture that teaches that freedom means self-assertive and radical autonomy from any external authority, this may seem to be weakness, even wimpishness. Jesus reveals a different, deeper truth about the human condition: that "whoever seeks to gain his life will lose it, but whoever loses his life will preserve it" (*Luke* 17.33).

Getting the Story Straight

Another way to think about that original sin—and the human condition—is to think of it as a question of humanity losing its script, forgetting its story.[13] History then becomes the quest to recover, or remember, that lost story line. None of us can live without a story, a narrative of where we came from and where we're heading, within which our lives make sense to us. When the Catholic Church teaches that Jesus Christ is "the center of the universe and of history," the Church is not boasting idly about the founder of the firm.[14] It is making a proposal about the world's true story—and it is suggesting how each of us fits into that narrative.

To think of Christ as the center of the universe and of history is to look at the world in a different and evocative way. Through the prism of faith we learn that world history and what believers call "salvation history" do not run on parallel tracks. Rather, in the Catholic view of things salvation history—the story of God's encounter with history, which reaches its dramatic climax in Jesus Christ—*is* world history, read in its true depth. Salvation history, God's search for us, is the inner dynamic of the human story, the engine of human history.

In a way, it's a question of which chapter headings make most sense. It's certainly possible to organize the human story under chapter headings that read "Prehistoric Man," "Ancient Civilizations," "The Greeks and the Romans," "The Dark Ages," "The Medieval World," "Renaissance and Reformation," "Enlightenment and Revolution," "The Modern World," "The Space Age." But do we get to the deeper truths about humankind, its origins, and its destiny through that kind of narrative? The Catholic proposal is that the richer, ampler, truer telling of the human story is organized under a different set of chapter headings: "Creation," "Fall," "Promise," "Prophecy," "Incarnation," "Redemption," "Sanctification," "The Kingdom of God."

The pivot of that story, the "center of the universe and of

history," is Jesus Christ. His story is the story that makes ultimate sense out of our individual stories and of the whole human drama. This is the Catholic claim in all its daring specificity: that at a certain time, in a certain place, and acting through real human lives, the Creator of the universe entered his creation in order to redirect the human story back toward its true destiny, which is eternal life with God. The Son of God who became incarnate in the womb of a Jewish girl, in an obscure village on the fringes of the Roman Empire some two thousand years ago, draws humanity into the inner life of God—and in doing so dramatically changes the possibilities in the human condition. When the Son of God becomes man, the past, like the present and the future, is forever caught up in the great drama of God's creative, redeeming, and sanctifying purposes. In entering the world for the salvation of the world, which is the world's destiny and future, Christ makes "history" possible by ensuring that what is past will not disappear into a black hole of nothingness.

That is why the Second Vatican Council taught that nothing genuinely human fails to find an echo in Christian hearts.[15] Everything that is, is of interest, because everything is part of the epic of creation and redemption. Everyone who is, is of infinite value, because every human being is a player in a great cosmic drama with eternal consequences—a drama in which God is both playwright and protagonist.

In preaching Jesus Christ, the Church is proposing an encounter and an interpretation: an encounter with the God who frees us from the dark confusion of questions without answers and an interpretation of history's origin and destiny. At the center of both the encounter and the interpretation is radical, self-giving love. For "God is love, and he who abides in love abides in God, and God in him" (*1 John* 4.16). At the bottom of the cosmos we do not find chemicals and gases, entropy and the coldness of nothingness and death; at the bottom of history we do not find randomness or chaos. At the root of the cosmos and of history is love.

And love is "the most living thing . . . there is."[16]

An Outrage?

Is it an outrage for the Catholic Church to propose that this Christ-centered story is not merely an interesting story, perhaps even a noble story, but in fact *the* story of the human condition and of human history? Isn't that a bit over the top? Doesn't it promote narrowness, intolerance, even hatred to propose that Jesus Christ is uniquely the world's "savior"—the definitive, unique, unsurpassable revelation of God's purposes for the world and for history, the one in whom we find our way home?

Although those concerns have a contemporary ring to them, they are, in fact, quite old. The Roman emperor Julian (331–363) harshly criticized Judaism and Christianity for their intolerance of other gods. The first commandment given to Israel, that Israel must have "no other gods" but the God who revealed himself on Sinai (*Exodus* 20.3), was Emperor Julian's chief complaint against Christianity and his single complaint against Judaism. Refusing to recognize the uniqueness of the one God, the man whom history remembers as Julian the

Apostate argued that the God of Israel was only one appearance of what he termed the "great mystery." To think otherwise, he insisted, was illiberal, unintelligent—in a word, intolerant.

Evidence to the contrary, however, was abundant and could be found everywhere in the late Roman world. For Christianity "made it" in the Roman Empire not only because of the forcefulness of its doctrine but because that doctrine empowered the people of the time, especially women, to lead better, happier, more secure, and more tolerant lives. The Jesus movement created networks of affection, social welfare, and health care across the rigid class and ethnic barriers of Roman society. It gave new dignity to women by celebrating marriage and rejecting infanticide, usually practiced against baby girls. It nurtured the belief that children were more than property. It made sense out of omnipresent physical suffering and the seeming randomness of life, creating islands of stability amid the chronic chaos of Roman cities. In short, the Jesus movement succeeded because it broke through the narrowness and intolerance characteristic of pagan antiquity. It did that by providing a compelling alternative lifestyle to the cruelty and venality of Roman times, so amply displayed in the award-winning film *Gladiator*.[17]

That belief in the uniqueness of Christ as the world's savior inevitably leads to intolerance is a charge contradicted by many Christian witnesses in the modern world. Mother Teresa of Calcutta did not become an international icon of selfless generosity despite her belief in Jesus Christ, the only Son of God and the unique savior of the world; she lifted the wretched human refuse of Calcutta's hard streets out of the gutters and loved them unto death because of her faith in Christ. For each of those untouchables, she insisted, was "Jesus in a particularly disturbing disguise." Similarly, if on a different plane, Pope John Paul II has become a leading exponent of international human rights, interreligious dialogue, and reconciliation because of his Christian faith, not despite it. As he put it in his first encyclical, *Redemptor Hominis* [The Redeemer of Man], the Catholic Church must exhibit a "universal openness," so that "all may be able to find in her 'the unsearchable riches of Christ'" of which St. Paul wrote (*Ephesians* 3.8).[18] Tolerance, the Pope was suggesting, does not mean avoiding differences, on the ground that there is "your truth" and "my truth" but nothing that both of us could ever recognize as *the* truth. Genuine tolerance means exploring and engaging differences, especially differences about ultimate things, within a bond of profound respect—a respect for all those whose very humanity compels them to search for answers to the deepest questions of life.[19] That is the respect demanded by Catholic faith.

That Catholics have been intolerant, to the point of coercion and bloodshed, is obvious from history. That the Church acknowledges those failures and recognizes that they were a betrayal of Christ and his Gospel is what John Paul II underscored on the First Sunday of Lent during the jubilee year of 2000, when he led the entire Catholic Church in a great act of repentance for the failures of the past two millennia. Critics within the Church complained that confessing the sins of the Church's sons and daughters weakened Catholicism. John Paul, a wiser student of theology and history, understood that confession was essential if the Church was to enter the third millennium of its history strengthened in its faith about the unique saving mission of Jesus Christ and convinced that the way of Christ was the way of persuasion, not coercion.

Living Beyond Fear

The Christ whom Catholicism preaches as the one savior of the world is, according to long-settled Christian doctrine, "true God and true man." His humanity was not a costume in which his divinity presented itself. His humanity was real, substantial, complete. And so he knew fear. One of the most wrenching scenes in the Gospels depicts Jesus in an agony of fear the night before his death. He sensed the awfulness that was coming; he feared it; and he prayed that God might "let this cup pass from me" (*Matthew* 26:39).

The agony of Jesus in the garden of Gethsemane has seemed to many commentators, Christian and otherwise, a profound metaphor for the human condition today. One theologian writes that in the contemporary world, "Fear mercilessly grips the human throat. It fills the psychiatrists' consulting rooms, populates the psychiatric hospitals, increases the suicide figures, lays blast-bombs, sets off cold wars and hot wars. We try to root it out of our souls like weeds, anesthetizing ourselves with optimism, trying to persuade ourselves with a forced philosophy of hope; we make all possible stimulants available . . . we invite people to engage in every form of self-alienation."[20] The richer, healthier, and better-traveled some affluent people become, the less secure, it seems, they are. The more a shrinking planet brings people of different cultures into close proximity, the more fearful of one another they become.

The Catholic faith in Jesus Christ does not deny fear, any more than Jesus denied his fear in that garden on the outskirts of Jerusalem almost two thousand years ago. Faith transforms fear through a personal encounter with Jesus Christ and his cross. In his free and complete surrender to God's will, Jesus took all the world's fear with him onto the cross and offered that fear, along with himself, to God. God's answer to that came on Easter, in the resurrection of Christ, the ultimate conquest of the final fear that is death.

The Christian does not live without fear or against fear. The Christian lives beyond fear. That trait is exemplified in Pope John Paul II. The Yugoslav dissident writer Milovan Djilas, who had seen a lot of fearful things in his life, once said that what most struck him about John Paul II was that the Pope was utterly without fear.[21] John Paul's fearlessness, it must be underlined, is distinctively Christian in character. It is not a stoic fearlessness, a brave defiance of an essentially irrational world. It is not a fearlessness that comes from being completely free of personal moral duties and personal obligations to others. And it is most certainly not a delusional fearlessness, a denial of all the things that make the modern world and its people afraid. The Pope's fearlessness is unmistakably Christian: which is to say, it is unmistakably Christ-centered. That was why, on his last day in Jerusalem in March 2000, John Paul II, then almost eighty years old, a man who walks with difficulty and pain, insisted on climbing the steep stone steps up to Calvary, the site of Christ's crucifixion, within the Church of the Holy Sepulchre. He wanted to pray at the place where all human fear was offered by the Son of God to his Father, an offering that made it possible for all humanity to live without fear.

That is what Catholicism means by "redemption." And because he is the redeemer, Jesus Christ is the answer to the question that is every human life.

2

Does Belief in God Demean Us?

Liberation and the God of Abraham, Isaac, Jacob, and Jesus

Is the God whom Jesus called "Father" an enemy of freedom? Does faith in the God of the Bible somehow demean and diminish us? Will humanity remain superstitious and immature until it frees itself of the "need" for God? These modern questions—and the positive answers often given to them—have dramatically changed the face of our world.

Throughout most of the developed world, Sunday looks very different than it did even sixty or seventy years ago. The crisis of faith embodied in empty churches in Europe and Canada, and in diminished Catholic practice in the United States, has many causes. Some people are bored by religious institutions. Others are genuinely skeptical that human beings can know the truth of anything, much less the truth of ultimate things. The Church's own failures to proclaim the Gospel persuasively and the imperfect lives of Christians also loom large in understanding the sources of disbelief, or simple lack of interest, today.

In these three respects—boredom, skepticism, the Church's own limitations—our contemporary situation replicates two thousand years of Christian history. Still, there is something dramatically new in the modern crisis of faith: the notion that the biblical God is an enemy of human maturity and human freedom. Some people have always found the institutional Church difficult to embrace; some people are innately skeptical; the Church is always less than it should be as a witness to Christ. The really new and distinctively modern charge is that, even if the Church were an effective, compelling, persuasive witness, what it proclaims is inherently dehumanizing. That is the contemporary indictment of the God of the Bible. And it has had an immense impact on the history of our times.

During the Second World War, one of the wisest theologians of the twentieth century, the French Jesuit Henri de Lubac (1896–1991), tried to trace the singular terrors of the twentieth century back to their roots. What, he asked, had produced communism, Nazism, and that gross utilitarianism that reduces human beings to objects for economic or political manipulation? De Lubac was a man who believed that ideas have consequences. His answer was that, in one way or another, the evils of the twentieth century were the products of something genuinely new in human affairs—something he called "atheistic humanism."[1]

Atheism was, of course, nothing new. The village atheist and the radically skeptical intellectual were familiar figures. Atheistic humanism had different characteristics. This was not the skepticism of individuals or the boredom of men and women turned off by the Church as an institution. This was atheism with a developed ideology and a program for remaking the world. Its prophets, who included some of the most prominent intellectuals of the nineteenth century, all taught that the God of the Bible was an enemy of human dignity and of freedom. Novelist Franz Werfel captured the flavor of this new kind of atheism in *The Song of Bernadette*. In mid-nineteenth-century Lourdes, a village in the French Pyrenees, the supernatural is stubbornly trying to reassert itself through miraculous cures. This offends M. Duran, a café keeper and leader of the local party of atheistic humanism. In M. Duran's view, all rational men ought to agree on certain obvious propositions:

> [T]he organization of nature [is] a relatively simple thing. Heaven is empty and rigid space dotted by some billions of sidereal systems. . . . In the immeasurable voids between the globes of fire there was evidently no place for the so-called supernatural. On a minor satellite of one of the least of those sidereal systems there vegetates an ape-like creature called man. The notion that a male of this animal species, above all one of its wretched females, could be the image of beings who rule . . . the universe, this could be but the ideology of such primitive savages as had not yet won man's first, if not also his final, victory—the renunciation of wishful dreams. Not until this sad and intentional stupidity at the basis of all illusionism was overcome; not until man had liberated himself from the immemorial emotional delusion that he and his earth were the centre of things and his mind something other than a purposeful function of matter determined by necessity; to sum up, not until he resigns

> himself to see his life in its true colours of a physico-chemico-biological mechanism, not until then will he begin at last to be a human being instead of a semi-animal haunted by demonic dreams. This evolution toward a truly human status will inevitably issue in tolerance, the rule of reason, and the annihilation of all dark and aggressive instincts.[2]

These ideas and this program constituted a great reversal, Henri de Lubac argued. The ancient world had experienced biblical religion as liberation from the whimsies of Fate. If God had created the world and the men and women who inhabited it, and if each human being had a direct link to the Creator through worship and prayer, then human beings could no longer be manipulated by countless gods, spirits, and demons who played games with our lives. The biblical God, by contrast to the ancient world's deities, was neither a willful tyrant nor a philosophical abstraction. Nor was he a remote, cosmic watchmaker, content to create the world and then leave it to its own devices. The God of Abraham, Isaac, Jacob, and Jesus had entered history and had become our companion on the pilgrimage of life. To be in communion with this God was to be liberated from Fate, liberated for freedom, liberated for human excellence.

But what Judaism and Christianity proposed as liberation, atheistic humanism called bondage. Getting rid of God, M. Duran and thousands like him argued, was the precondition to human greatness. This was not the atheism of the intellectually fashionable or the atheism of despair. This was atheistic humanism, on the march in the name of human liberation. And according to Father de Lubac, it was at the heart of the civilizational crisis of the twentieth century.

For this new idea had not remained simply an idea. Brought into history by Lenin, Hitler, Mao, and their lesser imitators, atheistic humanism had taught a lethal lesson. Once it was thought that human beings could not organize the world without God. That, Father de Lubac conceded, was not true; as the twentieth century amply demonstrated, human beings could certainly try to organize their lives and affairs entirely on their own. What atheistic humanism had proven was that, without God, human beings could organize the world only in a brutal contest of wills, one against another. That was the terrible lesson of atheistic humanism in its fascist, communist, and utilitarian forms. Exclusive, ultramundane humanism is inevitably inhuman humanism. In the suffocating climate of a world without windows or doors, human beings inevitably turn on one another.

The catastrophes that atheistic humanism caused in the twentieth century raise some urgent and interesting questions. Might it be that the opposite of the skeptics' claim is true? Might it be that the man or woman most dependent on God is, precisely because of that, most free as a human being? Suppose our dependence on God and our human freedom grow in direct proportion?

Rumors of Angels

Once upon a time, and indeed not so very long ago, reasonably well educated Catholics could list what were called the "proofs" for the existence of God: God as the "Prime Mover," the "Uncaused Cause," the "Necessary Being," and so forth.[3] Today, though the Catholic Church still teaches that the fact of God's existence can be rationally known, the Church's notion of proofs has been refined. "The person who seeks God," the *Catechism of the Catholic Church* suggests, "discovers certain ways of coming to know him. These are . . . called proofs for the existence of God, not in the sense of proofs in the natural sciences, but rather in the sense of 'converging and convincing arguments.' "[4] We become convinced of the truth of God's existence not as we become convinced that two plus two always equals four in the base-ten system, but as we become convinced that we love and are loved by someone. What the *Catechism* calls "converging and convincing arguments" for the reality of God emerge not from abstraction, but from our experience of the world and of our own lives.

Thirty-some years ago, a sociologist, Peter L. Berger, offered a winsome demonstration of this. In a book that became a small classic, entitled *A Rumor of Angels,* Professor Berger argued that there are "signals of transcendence" embedded in the human condition, moments that powerfully suggest that the world of our sensory experience is not all there is. These signals of transcendence are part of the natural world and our common experience, but they "appear to point beyond that reality" toward something that might plausibly be called the "supernatural." Berger's signals of transcendence don't have to do with extraordinary spiritual experiences, like the raptures and torments of great mystics. They emerge from the common, everyday realities of life.

Take, for example, the human need for order. Human

beings cannot live without order. We are terrified by chaos, and rather than live in political chaos, men and women will choose to live under an efficient tyranny (as, for example, in Germany in the early 1930s). Our need for order, however, is not just social and political. It is deeply personal, even interpersonal. Berger asks us to think about a mother reassuring a frightened child. Imagine a child awakened at night by a bad dream, shocked into a world that seems dark and threatening. When the child cries out, the mother responds. What does she say to comfort the child? Invariably, Berger writes, "the content of this communication . . . [is] the same—'Don't be afraid—everything is in order, everything is all right.'"

The mother, we see, is not simply addressing the immediate situation. She is making a statement about reality itself, a reality that transcends the immediate fright of her child: "*Everything* is all right." Berger suggests that this familiar statement of reassurance is a "rumor of angels"—a signal of transcendence with cosmic implications. For to say, instinctively, "Everything is all right," implies two things: that the "order" a mother brings to a frightened child is related to an "order that transcends it," and that this transcendent reality is something to which we can trust ourselves and our futures.

Then there is the experience of play. Berger describes little girls playing hopscotch in a park: "They are completely intent on their game, closed to the world outside it, happy in their concentration. Time has stood still for them. . . . The outside world has, for the duration of the game, ceased to exist. And, by implication (since the little girls may not be very conscious of this), pain and death, which are the law of that world, have also ceased to exist. Even the adult observer of this scene, who is perhaps all too conscious of pain and death, is momentarily drawn into the beatific immunity." The girls' play takes place in a time dimension of its own, a time out of time—or if you will, a time beyond time. The experience of being "in" that time out of time is a signal of transcendence. Play teaches us that the time we know is not all the time there is, and learning that is liberating.

Peter Berger goes on to discuss three other rumors of angels, or signals of transcendence, that emerge from the "normal" world even as they point beyond it. There is the experience of "hope beyond death," manifest in the courage of a soldier who sacrifices himself for a comrade, or the commitment of a dissident who says what he knows he must say, despite the dire consequences. There is the experience of absolute revulsion we feel at certain crimes that seem to "cry out to heaven" (and hell). And there is our experience of the comic; our laughter at the incongruities and absurdities of life (what Berger calls "the imprisonment of the human spirit in the world") points beyond the tragic to a liberated, even redeemed, future.

Our lives, Professor Berger concludes, are full of ecstasy: not in the sense of extraordinary mystical experiences, but in the quite ordinary sense of all those moments in which we step "outside the taken-for-granted reality of everyday life" and experience an "openness to the mystery that surrounds us."[5] The daily rhythms of life, Berger suggests, tell us that we don't live in a closed universe but in a world with windows and doors. Certain realities of our daily lives disclose a reality beyond our daily lives, and that is as true for ordinary people as it is for mystics. That transcendent reality, the "mystery" that surrounds our world, the presence of which we can detect in our world, is the mystery that Christians call "God." When we encounter that reality, the human condition seems lighter, freer, more of an opportunity and less of a burden; tomorrow seems an occasion for expectation, not fear. In encountering the mystery of God, we find liberation, not bondage.

God: Fatherhood and Mercy

Experiences of transcendence are all around us, and as the *Catechism of the Catholic Church* proposes, some careful reflection on those experiences can add up to a set of "converging and convincing arguments" for the reality of God. Those experiences cannot tell us all that much about who God is, however, or what God's attributes might be. For that knowledge, the Catholic Church teaches, we must look to the data of revelation, which is God's self-revelation. Where does the biblical God let us know who he is? God tells us who he is in history: through his relationship with his chosen people, Israel, and through his Son, Jesus Christ, who reveals God's attributes in his person, his teaching, and his actions.

Writing on the "character" of God as revealed in the Hebrew Bible and the New Testament, Pope John Paul II stresses above all God's mercy, which is the essential attribute of God's fatherhood. Throughout the Hebrew Bible, from the rebellion at Mt. Sinai to the settlement of the land of Israel to the trials, exile, and return of the Jewish people, God constantly makes himself known, amid his people's inconstancy and infidelity, by his constancy and fidelity: God makes himself known through his mercy. The Hebrew Bible emphasizes that the God of Abraham, Isaac, and Jacob is a just God. The Hebrew scriptures also reveal, according to John Paul II, that "love is 'greater' than justice: greater in the sense that it is primary and fundamental."[6]

The theme of God's faithful, unbounded mercy continues in the teaching of Jesus, most poignantly and powerfully in the parable of the prodigal son. This story (*Luke* 15.11–32), which is more aptly called the parable of the merciful father, is a synthesis of the entire biblical theology of mercy—and thus a synthesis of the biblical portrait of God. As John Paul II explains the parable, the prodigal son (who leaves his father's house and wastes his inheritance on a dissolute life of self-indulgence) is a universal figure, an Everyman feeling the full weight of the human condition: "the awareness of squandered sonship," our lost human dignity. By restoring his repentant son to his house, not (as the son proposes) as a hireling but as a member of the family, the forgiving father is faithful to his paternity, John Paul writes. As "father," he goes beyond the strict norms of justice and restores to his wayward son the truth about himself—the dignity of being a son, which he has lost. True mercy, the parable suggests, does not humiliate the one who receives it. By confirming the recipient of divine mercy in his or her human dignity, God liberates us.[7]

The God whom Jesus reveals is far more than a cosmic assurance that everything that is, including our own lives, is not the result of sheer contingency. The reality of God means that we do not live in an irrational or absurd world, and knowing that is very important. By means of God's self-disclosure in the history of Israel and in Jesus Christ, we know so much more.

The God whom Jesus reveals is God as Father, God as paternal mercy, in whom justice and love meet, liberating those on whom that mercy falls. To seek out that God is neither childish nor demeaning. To seek out the Father of mercies is to recognize our neediness for what it is, and to recognize ourselves for who we are. That is the path of maturity. It is also the path of authentic freedom.

The Trinity

For almost two millennia, Christians have struggled with the doctrine that the God of Abraham, Isaac, Jacob, and Jesus is a Trinity of Persons, whom Christians call "Father," "Son," and "Holy Spirit." The *Catechism of the Catholic Church* frankly confesses that in "his inmost Being as Holy Trinity," God "is a mystery that is inaccessible to reason alone."[8] Christians believe in God as a Trinity of Persons not because they thought their way to the doctrine of the Holy Trinity abstractly, but because of the Christian experience of God's "triune" revelation of himself: the Son reveals the Father, who sent the Son into the world; the Holy Spirit continues the Son's work in the world and in the Church, deepening our understanding of both the Father and the Son.

The intellectual difficulties of thinking about one God who is three Persons have challenged the most agile theological minds for centuries. The Trinity is also a conundrum for preachers, as St. Patrick, who according to pious legend tried to explain the Trinity to the Irish in the fifth century through the device of a shamrock, understood. Go into any Catholic church in the world on Trinity Sunday (which falls just one week after Pentecost, the great annual celebration of the Holy Spirit and the "birthday of the Church," celebrated fifty days after Easter) and, more likely than not, you'll hear the priest or deacon begin his sermon by saying, "This is the hardest week of the year in which to preach." But there is a way to talk about the Trinity that is accessible to nontheologians—and that further illustrates the point that faith in God teaches us important truths about human liberation.

Throughout the year, in its weekly and daily worship, the Church relives through readings from the Bible the great deeds that God did for his people. The Hebrew Bible teaches us that God created the world and gave humanity a singular place in his grand design. He chose a people, Israel, to be the bearers of his promise of liberation and redemption. In the fullness of time, the New Testament teaches, God sent his Son, born of the Virgin Mary, to take upon himself the sins of the world and to consume them in the fire of his self-sacrificing love. God then raised Jesus from the dead, and by doing so destroyed death's power over creation.

Each of these deeds was done by a God who does not remain aloof and alone but who is always with us. What God does teaches us something important about who God is. For God could not be "with us"—God could not enter into relationships of intimacy with men and women in history—if "being with" were not somehow part of the character of God in himself.

The God of Abraham, Isaac, Jacob, and Jesus is a God of loving intimacy with his creation. To be that kind of God for us, God must have an experience of loving intimacy, of "being with," in his own life. To teach us self-giving and receptivity and reciprocity, God must know these things in his own eternal life. The God whom Christians believe to be a Holy Trinity is a God overflowing with self-giving: the self-giving of the Father begets the Son, and the self-giving between Father and Son gives birth to a radical unity between Father and Son to whom the New Testament gives the name of "Holy Spirit."

Humanity began to glimpse this inner mystery of God's life through the mission of Jesus Christ, whom St. Matthew's Gospel calls by the Hebrew name Emmanuel, which means "God-with-us" in history. The incarnation of Jesus Christ, the Word of God become man, prompts our first intuition that "being with" is what God has been about for all eternity: God has "been with" from before the creation of the world. For what the Bible calls "creation" is the outpouring of God's interior vitality into time and history. The incarnation of Jesus Christ and the redemption he won for the world were Trinitarian acts, born from the superabundance of God's own giving, God's receptivity, God's reciprocity.

Put another way, perhaps an even deeper way, the truth about God the Holy Trinity is that God is a living, eternal event, a community of self-giving love and receptivity. We can glimpse this profound truth about the life of God-in-himself through our experience of God-with-us. God's deeds in history are a divine invitation to ponder, in awe, the love that is God-in-himself, a Trinity of Persons in a unity of divinity.

God entered history in his chosen people, Israel, and in his Son, Jesus Christ, to "be with" us so that we might "be with" God for eternity. That, in Christian belief, is humanity's destiny. That is what the death and resurrection of Jesus Christ, the Son of God and second Person of the Trinity, won for us. That is the promise that is sealed with the gift of the Holy Spirit, the third Person of that Trinity. We are to live, forever, within the light and love, the giving and receiving, of the Holy Trinity. That is what Christians celebrate at Christmas, Easter, and Pentecost, the great annual feasts of God's acts in history.

And that is one crucial dimension of this challenging Christian doctrine of the Trinity. The Trinity, a doctrine about God, casts a penetrating light on the meaning and purpose of every human life.[9] The doctrine of the Trinity reinforces the Christian claim that self-giving and receptivity are the road to human flourishing.

God Beyond "Spirituality"

One hundred years ago, on the edge of the twentieth century, enlightened opinion confidently predicted that humanity would outgrow its "need" for religion by the turn of the third millennium. Entering the twenty-first century, three of the most powerful cultural forces on the world stage are religious: activist Islam, evangelical Protestantism, and Roman Catholicism. In trying to describe this unexpected phenomenon, contemporary enlightened opinion turns to psychological categories and regards religion (often dubbed "spirituality") as one possible answer to a widely felt need. In this perspective, Christianity is one subset of the widespread human phenomenon called "religion." This new fascination with spirituality should not be dismissed. Neither should it be confused with what Catholicism understands itself to be.

The idea that religion is the genus of which Christianity is the species (and Catholicism the subspecies) was invented by nineteenth-century liberal Protestant scholars of the history of religions. Despite its limitations, this school of thought did identify what seems to be a universal fact: the human openness to the transcendent, illustrated by Peter Berger's "rumors of angels." But Christianity has never understood itself as simply one example of something else. Christianity is different, and that difference is made clear by the Christian holiday with the most universal appeal—Christmas. Many of those engaged in various forms of spirituality today understand religion as the human search for God; so do some Christians. In the Catholic view of things, though, Christianity is God's search for us, and our taking the same path as God does.[10]

That is what the Christmas story teaches us, for that is what the angels announced to the shepherds in the fields above Bethlehem. God had become man so that God might enter fully into the world's sorrow, transforming it to joy. The shepherds are invited to undertake this journey, to go to meet God, who is to be found "wrapped in swaddling clothes and lying in a manger" (*Luke* 2.7).

That curiosity—the Son of God submitting his freedom to human binding in order to set us free—is but the first of the sometimes disturbing surprises presented by the story of God incarnate, God in search of us. The drama of those surprises will intensify between Christmas and Good Friday, as the baby of Bethlehem becomes a sign of contradiction to a world that rejects him, abuses him, and ultimately kills him. The mystery does not end with death, though. The Son's complete self-sacrifice is vindicated by the Father in the resurrection of Jesus, who as Christ the risen Lord sends forth his Holy Spirit so that we may be free as he is free.

God in search of us is not just an example of religion. It is not another episode in spirituality. It is, the Catholic Church proposes, nothing less than the truth of the world.

3

Liberal Church? Conservative Church?

Why Catholicism Is Not a "Denomination," and What That Means

On January 25, 1959, Pope John XXIII shocked the Catholic world by announcing his intention to summon the twenty-first ecumenical Council in the history of the Church. The previous twenty Councils had defined dogma, condemned heresy, written legal codes, and deposed emperors. They had tried, unsuccessfully, to heal the divisions between the Christian East and the Christian West; they had established guidelines for worship and penitential practice. Ecumenical Councils of all the world's bishops had met in Italy, France, Germany, and Asia Minor; they had lasted a few months, and in one case, eighteen years. Whatever they accomplished, wherever they had met, or however long they had taken, virtually all of the ecumenical Councils had been caused by controversy, conducted in controversy, and followed by controversy.

John XXIII had something different in mind.

The seventy-eight-year-old Pope imagined the Council as a "new Pentecost." Just as the Holy Spirit, on the first Pentecost, had empowered the apostles to preach the truth of Jesus Christ in Jerusalem and throughout the Roman Empire, the Second Vatican Council, as Pope John envisioned it, would be a great Spirit-led experience that would reconstitute the Catholic Church as a dynamic evangelical movement in history. This new kind of Council would not issue dogmatic definitions, nor would it condemn heresies. Rather, it would be an open-ended conversation among the world's bishops on renewing Catholicism as a vital and compelling way of life. John XXIII seemed to think that too much attention had been paid in recent centuries to the Church as institution. It was time to reimagine the Church as an *evangelical movement.* Structures had their place, but their place was to serve the Church-as-movement as it proclaimed the astonishing news of God's passionate love affair with the world he had created.

Some of what John XXIII hoped for actually happened.

In the decades after Vatican II, Catholicism in Africa, Asia, and parts of Latin America has been renewed as a vibrant evangelical enterprise. Renewal movements in those parts of the world, and in Europe and North America, are creating new forms of Christian community, witness, and service. Some things that could not have been anticipated also happened, though. Previously vital Catholic communities—in the Netherlands, Belgium, Germany, France, Spain, Portugal, Ireland, Switzerland, and Québec—imploded and then disintegrated. Western Europe today is the most religiously arid place on the planet. Once vibrantly Catholic Québec is the most secularized region between the North Pole and Tierra del Fuego.

Whether this dramatic decline in traditional centers of Catholic vitality happened because of Vatican II, despite Vatican II, or independently of Vatican II is a question that will not be answered for decades, perhaps even centuries. The answer, when it comes into focus, will likely include elements of all three explanations. What can be said with certainty now is that, since John XXIII called Catholicism to a richer, more evangelical way of imagining itself and its purposes, an almost obsessive focus on the Catholic Church as institution has preoccupied many Catholics in North America and western Europe.

That obsession with the institutional dimension of the Church helps to explain why so much of the contemporary Catholic debate is framed in terms borrowed from politics: as a debate between "liberals" and "conservatives." Shortly after the Council, virtually everything in Catholicism began to be described this way. There were liberal and conservative bishops, priests, nuns, parishes, religious orders, seminaries, theologians, newspapers, magazines, and organizations. There were liberal and conservative positions on every question imaginable, from the structure of worship to the fine points of doctrine and morality.

To be sure, there was something to all this. Some Catholics eagerly welcomed the revision of the Church's worship; others were offended, appalled, or heart-stricken by "the changes." Some Catholics were entirely comfortable in the dialogue with modern culture; others thought that opening the Church's windows to the modern world was a grave mistake; still others welcomed the new conversation but thought the Church should challenge the modern world to open its windows, too. The liberal/conservative grid was moderately useful for sorting out some of the players and a few of the issues during and immediately after Vatican II.

But the use of the liberal/conservative filter as a one-size-fits-all template for thinking about an ancient, complex religious institution was, in the final analysis, implausible and distorting. An example from another world religion illustrates why. No one ever asks whether the Dalai Lama is a liberal or conservative Buddhist. Why? Because we instinctively understand that these are the wrong categories through which to grasp the nature and purpose of a venerable, subtle, and richly textured religious tradition. Shouldn't the same self-discipline be applied to thinking about the Catholic Church?

In the United States, the liberal/conservative filter has also reinforced the temptation to think of Catholicism as one among many "denominations." American religion, it is often said, is preeminently denominational religion. What much of American Christianity means by "denomination," though, is not what Catholicism means by "Church."

There is little that is given or secure in a denomination; the denomination is constantly being remade by its members. Christianity as denomination has no distinctive, fixed *form,* given to it by Christ; it adapts its form, its institutional structures, to the patterns of the age. (To take a current example, if the basic institutional form of the wider society is the bureaucracy, the Church becomes identified with its bureaucracy.) In much of American denominational Christianity today, institutional process is more important than binding doctrinal reference points; anything can change. The denominational community's boundaries are ill defined, even porous, because being nonjudgmental is essential to group maintenance. Religious leadership is equated with bureaucratic managership; bishops and other formally constituted religious leaders are discussion moderators whose job is to keep all opinions in play, rather than authoritative teachers.

A denomination is something we help create by joining it; according to Vatican II, however, the Church is a divinely instituted community into which we are incorporated by the sacraments of initiation (baptism, confirmation, the Eucharist). Denominations have members like voluntary associations or clubs; the Church has members as a human body has arms and legs, fingers and toes. A denomination has moving boundaries, doctrinally and morally; the Church, according to Vatican II, is nourished by creeds and moral convictions that clearly establish its boundaries. The structures of a denomination are something we can alter at will; the Church, according to Vatican II, has a form, or structure, given to it by Christ. Catholicism has bishops and a ministerial priesthood, and Peter's successor, the Bishop of Rome, presides over the whole Church in charity, not because Catholics today think these are good ways to do things but because Christ wills these for his Church.

None of this distinctively Catholic way of thinking about the Church makes much sense if parsed in liberal/conservative terms. Better categories, rooted in a richer concept of the Church than the Church as institution, have to be found.

THE CHURCH AS A "COMMUNION"

What do we mean by "Church"? The bishops of Vatican II, having searched extensively through the Hebrew Bible and the New Testament, proposed a host of biblical metaphors to describe the essence of the Church and its mission. The Council's *Dogmatic Constitution on the Church* describes the Church of Christ in these agrarian images: "This Church is . . . a sheepfold, the sole and necessary gateway to which is Christ (cf. *John* 10.1–10). It is also the flock, of which God foretold that he himself would be the shepherd (cf. *Isaiah* 40.11; *Ezekiel* 34.11ff.), and whose sheep, although watched over by human shepherds, are nevertheless at all times led and brought to pasture by Christ himself, the Good Shepherd and prince of shepherds (cf. *John* 10.11; *1 Peter* 5.4), who gave his life for his sheep (cf. *John* 10.11–15)."

The Second Vatican Council also cited biblical images drawn from architecture to describe the Church. Thus the Church is the "building of God" (*1 Corinthians* 3.9) whose cornerstone is Christ (*Matthew* 21.42). Built by the apostles on the one "foundation" which is Jesus Christ (*1 Corinthians* 3.11), the Church is the "household of God in the Spirit (cf. *Ephesians* 2.19–22), the dwelling place of God among men (*Revelation* 21.3), and, especially, the holy temple. . . . As living stones, we here on earth are built into it (cf. *1 Peter* 2.5)." The Church is also proposed as the "holy city," and the holy city is variously described as "the Jerusalem which is above" (*Galatians* 4.26) and the "spotless spouse of the Lamb" (*Revelation* 19.7), whom Christ "loved and for whom he delivered himself that he might sanctify her" (*Ephesians* 5.25–26).[1]

The Council adopted this rich biblical imagery in an effort to get Catholics to think of themselves in something more than institutional terms. The biblical pyrotechnics in the *Dogmatic Constitution on the Church* are meant to help us imagine the Church and all its functions—including its necessary institutional functions—as a dynamic evangelical movement in history. That is what the Church is for, Pope John Paul II has insisted. The Church does not exist for her own sake. The Church exists to tell the world that "in the fullness of time, [God] sent his Son, born of a woman, for the salvation of the world." That means that "the history of salvation has entered the history of the world," and time has been incorporated into eternity. The story of salvation—the story of the Church, and the story of Israel that made the Church's story possible—*is* the world's story, rightly understood.

The primary mission of the Church is most certainly not institutional maintenance. The first mission of the Church is to tell the world the truth about itself, by means of what the Pope calls a "dialogue of salvation."[2] The Church exists to propose to the world: "You are far, far greater than you imagine."

If that is what the Church is for, that should tell us something about what the Church is. Because the Church, as Vatican II puts it, is "the kingdom of God now present in mystery," the Church cannot think of itself as one religious organization in a supermarket of religious options.[3] The Church, writes John Paul II, has a "unique importance for the human family," for the Church is where the human family learns the truth about its origins, dignity, and destiny.

The Church is also where we experience a foretaste of that destiny, which is eternal life within the light and love of the Holy Trinity.[4] That is why the Council, the Pope, and prominent Catholic theologians all suggest that the Church is best described as a *communion*—a communion of believers with the living God, with one another, and with the saints who have gone before us. Because the Church has a certain structure, the Church does certain things. So we can speak of the Church as institution, herald, servant, and so forth.[5] At the bottom of the bottom line, however, the Church is a *communion*. Those who participate in that communion—husbands and wives, parents and children, friends and colleagues, employers and employees—have a relationship to one another in that communion that is like none other in their lives. In all those other relationships, we are "part" of one another in different ways. Those in the communion of the Church are "part" of one another as parts of the Body of Christ.

The communion that is the Church extends over time and beyond time. In the Catholic view of things, the reality of the Church embraces far more than those we see around us in the world. It also, as John Paul puts it, "embraces those who now see God as he is, and those who have died and are being purified." Put yet another way, the distinctive quality of the communion of the Church is that it is a "communion of saints": those who are already saints (that is, those who "see God as he is") and those who must become saints in order to fulfill their Christian and human destiny (that is, all the rest of us).[6]

To think of the Church as a communion of saints means that we have to think differently about the meaning of *vocation.*

Called and Sent

Ask most Catholics what a vocation is and they're likely to respond, "Becoming a priest," or, "Becoming a nun." Those are surely vocations within the communion of the Church. Still, limiting the notion of vocation to those who are religious professionals is a mistake, according to the Second Vatican Council and Pope John Paul II.

If the Church is the continuation in time of Christ's mission and the mission of the Holy Spirit, then the Church's first task is evangelization—the sharing of the good news that God loves the world, gave his Son for the salvation of the world, and invites all humankind to a life of eternal happiness. That astonishingly good news demands to be shared. The Church, by its very nature, is missionary, and every baptized Christian has a responsibility—a vocation—to be an evangelist. The Council described this by saying that all the baptized share in Christ's vocation as prophet: every Christian shares in the prophetic mission of Christ by speaking the truth, by proposing to the world the truth about its story.

The Church's evangelization must be nurtured in prayer, especially community prayer. There is an intimate link between the Christian vocation to evangelize and the Christian vocation to worship. In worshiping the Father, through the Son, in the power of the Holy Spirit, the Church deepens its understanding of the truth about itself and is equipped for its mission in the world. All the baptized, according to Vatican II, share in Christ's vocation as priest: every Christian shares in the priestly mission to worship in truth, to give the Father what is his due, and to receive in return the gift of holy communion, in and with God's Son.

The Church's evangelization must be lived in service. Sometimes the Gospel message is best conveyed by deeds rather than by words. It is one thing, and an important thing, to preach that God loves the world and calls us to communion with him. That message is sometimes most effectively communicated by action, by lives of service poured out for others in imitation of Christ and in obedience to Christ. All the baptized share in Christ's vocation as king: every Christian is called to a royal life, which is essentially a life of service and self-giving.[7]

To be baptized, the Church teaches, is to be "baptized into Christ," to "put on Christ." That means that every Christian has a baptismal vocation to holiness. Sanctity, in Catholicism, is not just for the sanctuary. Sanctity is for everyone, for we must all become saints (whether or not we are publicly recognized as such after our deaths) in order to enjoy eternal life with God. Each of us, Catholicism teaches, has a vocation, a unique way in which we are to grow into holiness. Our vocation is the way in which we each live our distinctive Christian witness, and thus are fitted to become the kind of people who can live with God forever.[8]

Formed in the Image of Mary

Another primary and common characteristic of all those who are embraced by the communion of the Church is that they are all disciples. In the Catholic view of things, that means that everyone in the Church is formed in the image of a woman: Mary, mother of Jesus, the first of disciples and thus the "Mother of the Church."

Every year the Pope meets with the senior members of the Roman Curia, the Church's central bureaucracy, for an exchange of Christmas greetings. It's a formal occasion, rather far removed from the typical office Christmas party. Popes traditionally use the opportunity to review the year just past and suggest directions for the year ahead. On December 22, 1987, Pope John Paul II made this the occasion to drop something of a theological bombshell.

For some years, Catholic theologians had speculated about different "profiles," or "images," of the Church, drawn from prominent New Testament personalities. The missionary Church, the Church of proclamation, is formed in the image of the apostle Paul, the great preacher to the Gentiles. The Church of contemplation is formed in the image of the apostle John, who rested his head on Christ's breast at the Last Supper. The Church of office and jurisdiction is formed in the image of Peter, the apostle to whom Christ gave the keys of the kingdom of heaven. All of these images are in play in the Church all the time. Yet, in a Church accustomed for centuries to thinking of itself primarily in institutional terms, the Church formed in the image of Peter's authority and office has long seemed to take priority over all the rest.

Not so, suggested John Paul II, to what we can only assume were some rather startled senior churchmen. Mary was the first disciple, because Mary's "yes" to the angel's message had made possible the incarnation of the Son of God. The Church is the extension of Christ and his mission in history; in the image made famous by Pope Pius XII, the Church is the "Mystical Body of Christ." Mary's assumption into heaven was a preview of what awaits all those whom Christ will save. For all these reasons, John Paul proposed, Mary provides a defining profile of what the Church is, of how the men and women of the Church should live, and of what the eternal destiny of disciples will be.

This understanding of Mary and the Church challenges the institutional way in which many churchmen (and many Catholic laity) are used to thinking about themselves and their community. The "Marian profile," John Paul said, is even "more . . . fundamental" in Catholicism than the "Petrine profile." Though the two cannot be divided, the "Marian Church," the Church formed in the image of a woman and her discipleship, precedes, makes possible, and indeed makes sense of the "Petrine Church," the Church of office and authority formed in the image of Peter. That Petrine Church, the Pope continued, has no other purpose "except to form the Church in line with the ideal of sanctity already programmed and prefigured in Mary." John Paul argued that these two profiles were complementary, not in tension. He also insisted that the "Marian profile is . . . pre-eminent" and carried within it a richer meaning for every Christian's vocation.[9]

It was a striking message. Discipleship comes before authority in the Church because authority is to serve sanctity. In a Church of disciples, formed in the image of Mary, the first disciple, what is fundamental is the universal call to holiness. Everything else in the Church—including the work of those with authority in the Church—exists to foster the disciples' answer to that call.

This is not a liberal view of the Church and its mission. This is not a conservative view of the Catholic reality. This is a vision far beyond those categories.

Archaeology Teaches a Lesson

The Marian Church is the fundamental reality of the Church as a communion of disciples. Still, the Office of Peter is a crucial part of the Catholic Church. Getting at the core of its meaning requires analytic tools other than the usual political categories. The liberal/conservative debate about the papacy in recent decades has not shed very much light on the evangelical essence of Peter's mission, which continues in the popes. Perhaps archaeology helps.

Deep beneath St. Peter's Basilica in the Vatican are the *scavi*, a series of archaeological digs begun by Pope Pius XII during the Second World War in an attempt to find the tomb of the prince of the apostles, which ancient tradition had associated with that site. Archaeological digs don't yield irrefutable answers, like algebraic equations. Still, the best scholarly opinion is that we can say with a reasonable degree of certainty that the apostle's tomb has been found, almost directly under Bernini's bronze baldachino, whose wreathed columns frame the papal high altar beneath the great dome emblazoned with Christ's words *"Tu es Petrus et super hanc petram aedificabo ecclesiam meam et tibi dabo claves regni caelorum"* [You are Peter and upon this rock I will build my Church and I will give you the keys of the kingdom of heaven; see *Matthew* 16.18–19].

In the course of their explorations under St. Peter's, archaeologists found an enormous cemetery, a Christian necropolis dating back to the decades immediately following the life of Christ—the decades of the first evangelization of the Mediterranean world and its imperial capital, Rome. Pious Christians who died quietly at home, as well as those who died horrible deaths by torture during Roman persecutions, wanted to be buried near Peter. And so a small city of the dead arose on the Vatican hill, a half hour's walk from the Coliseum and the Roman Forum.

To get to the *scavi* you pass through St. Peter's Square with its distinctive obelisk, a granite monolith brought to Rome in A.D. 37 by the mad emperor Caligula. His nephew, Nero, made the obelisk one of the centerpieces of his circus. It is not improbable that Peter was martyred in that circus, and it could well be that the last thing he saw on this earth was that obelisk.

In the *scavi,* the tourist or pilgrim is about as close as it's possible to get to the apostolic origins of the Church. That experience poses the question of Peter, and his meaning for us, in a very sharp way.

The great challenge to Christian faith is the incarnation of the Son of God and his death for us upon the cross: "a stumbling block to Jews and folly to Gentiles," as St. Paul put it (*1 Corinthians* 1.23). As if to compound the challenge, Christ left the continuation of his ministry and mission in the hands of weak, mortal human beings; he made the weakest, most impetuous of the bunch the first among them (*Matthew* 16.18–19); and then he told Peter that the essence of his leadership was the service of his brethren, which would, in due course, cost him his life (*Luke* 22.32; *John* 21.18–19).

The *scavi* make us confront, face-to-face, this bold claim: that at a certain time and place, a real human being named Simon, son of a man named John, a fisherman from Capernaum in Galilee, became a personal friend of Jesus of Nazareth. In that friendship, Simon encountered the Son of God and was transformed—not into a superhero but into Peter, an apostle, a man equipped by the Holy Spirit for a mission of witness "to the ends of the earth" (*Acts* 13.47). To go through the *scavi* is to be confronted with the unavoidable and almost shocking particularity of Catholic faith: These were real people. They made real decisions. They had real fears, real passions, real loves, and real enemies. This is all for real.

The Church is not founded on a pious myth. The Church is built on the foundation of the apostles: the first witnesses to the resurrection and the first to tell the world the good news of God's decisive, redemptive intervention in human history.

Simon, the fisherman from Galilee, whose life and death can be touched down in the *scavi,* was a weak man, like every other Christian. Peter, who bore the office of the keys, was a man reborn and remade by the power of the Holy Spirit. His was not a transformation into worldly glory. The risen Christ had warned him, "When you are old, you will stretch out your hands and another will gird you and carry you where you do not wish to go" (*John* 21.18). That journey led to his own cross and, in the world's terms, to the burial ground that visitors now know as the *scavi.*

By emptying himself of himself, by making himself the instrument of the Holy Spirit, Peter became "the rock." For two thousand years, the gates of hell have not prevailed against the Church he was to lead. It really is an extraordinary proposal. Down in the *scavi,* one confronts the undeniable reality of the Church. That demands a decision.

Liberating Doctrine

The Office of Peter is primarily an evangelical office; the pope is a pastor and evangelist first and an ecclesiastical executive later. Part of the function of the papacy as an evangelical office is to safeguard the integrity of the Church's doctrine. This is often thought of as a disciplinary role, the pope cuffing wayward theologians and ordering them into line. If we think of the Church as a communion of disciples, however, it is easier to understand as paradox what at first glance seems to be contradiction. Doctrine, those defined truths which mark the boundaries of Catholicism, is in fact liberating.

Doctrine can seem changeless and dull, an inhibition to creativity. To think of doctrine in these terms, though, is to miss the relationship between tradition and innovation, the static and the dynamic, in the life of the Church. What can seem static in Christian doctrine in fact reflects the Church's internal dynamism and creates the impetus for the unfolding of new elements in Christian life. What can seem dead tradition is in fact the engine of development and innovation.

Take three examples.

The first is Scripture. The canon of Scripture is fixed; there will be no books added to the Old or New Testament. The fact that the Church does not add new books to the canon of Scripture does not make Scripture a dead letter, though. The canon insures that what is truly the Word of God can be received freshly and in its integrity by every generation of believers, inviting them to a deeper faith through the mediation of the Bible.

Then there is the Church's sacramental system. The sacraments—baptism and the Eucharist, for example—are not simply traditional rituals, performed because previous generations did so before us. The sacraments enable each new generation of Christians to experience the great mysteries of faith—the life, death, and resurrection of Jesus Christ—anew. Every day, the sacraments remind every generation of Christians that just on the far side of the ordinary—water, salt, and oil; bread and wine; marital love and fidelity—lies the extraordinary reality of a God who so loved the world he created that he entered that world, in his Son, to redirect the world's history back toward its true destiny, eternal life within the light and love of the Trinity.

Finally, there is the matter of authority. The Church's structures of pastoral authority are not intended to impede human creativity. Authority in the Church exists to insure that Christians do not settle for mediocrity. Authority in the Church is meant to help all Catholics hold themselves accountable to the one supreme "rule of faith," the living Christ. This, for example, is the great service that pastoral authority does for theology: it keeps theology from getting too pleased with its own cleverness and calls it to a love of truth.[10]

One of the great tasks of the Church in the twenty-first century will be to retrieve and renew the concept of tradition. In the distinctively Catholic understanding of the term, "tradition" (which from its Latin root, *traditio,* means "handing on") begins inside the very life of God the Holy Trinity.[11] That handing on—that radical giving which mysteriously enhances both giver and receiver—took flesh in the life of Christ and continues in the Church through the gift of the Holy Spirit. A venerable formula distinguishes between tradition, the living faith of the dead, and traditionalism, the dead faith of the living. Pope John Paul II's teaching on the Marian Church of disciples that makes possible (and makes sense of) the Petrine Church of jurisdiction and office is a good example of tradition's capacity to inspire innovative thinking. The great Marian doctrines set boundaries for Catholic faith. In doing so, they compel fresh thought and new insight into the riches of the Church's heritage and the mysteries of God's action in the world.

Doctrine is not excess baggage weighing Catholics down on the journey of faith. Doctrine is the vehicle that enables the journey to take place.

4

Where Do We Find the "Real World"?

Liturgy and the Extraordinary Ordinary

Two of the most bruising debates in the Catholic Church today involve the Church's worship, or to use a technical term that will recur below, the Church's *liturgy.* The first of these ongoing controversies involves the changes in the celebration of Mass that were introduced in the wake of the Second Vatican Council. The second is the more recent argument over whether the Church is authorized to ordain women to the ministerial priesthood. No one who has been engaged in these debates would ever describe them as tranquil or serene. That tells us something important about Catholicism and the Catholic view of the world.

The intensity of feeling aroused by these issues powerfully testifies to an abiding Catholic intuition: that the Church is most intensely the Church when it is gathered around the altar. As the *Catechism of the Catholic Church* puts it,

"Through the liturgy Christ, our redeemer and high priest, continues the work of redemption in, with, and through his Church."[1] What is at stake in the debates over the reform of the liturgy and the nature of the priesthood is nothing less than the essence of the Church. Evangelization and charity are what the Church is *for;* the Church *is* a communion of liturgical worship, because the Church is the Body of Christ, in which the priesthood is an office of both proclamation and service.[2]

These two issues further illustrate how those familiar liberal/conservative categories, with their stress on the Church as institution, are simply inappropriate in dealing with matters at the center of Catholic faith and life. The debates over the reform of the Church's worship and over the ordination of women to the ministerial priesthood are frequently conducted, and almost invariably reported, as struggles for power between the forces of progress and the forces of reaction. Those favoring rapid liturgical change, to the point of radical liturgical experimentation, and those who argue that the ordination of women is a pastoral necessity are deemed in line with Vatican II and the Church's "opening to the modern world." Those who have questions about the character or pace of liturgical change and who argue that the Church does not have the authority to change two thousand years of priestly tradition are thought to be fighting a rearguard action against the inevitable, or in the latter case accused of misogyny. Liturgical change and the question of women's ordination are usually thought of as issues of power.

In both instances, though, politics is emphatically not what is at stake. These issues engage the most profound questions about the nature of the Church and about the nature of reality itself. They are, in a word, *theological* questions, not political questions. If they are not discussed as such, the debate will get nowhere.

A better prism through which to see what is at stake here comes from Evelyn Waugh's *Men at Arms,* the first in a trilogy of novels about the Second World War. In one memorable scene the trilogy's protagonist, Guy Crouchback, a Catholic, is attending his first formal dinner as an officer-in-training of the Royal Corps of Halberdiers. The champagne is flowing freely, and amid the post-dinner skits and games, Guy finds himself in conversation with the regiment's Anglican chaplain. "Do you agree," Guy asks, "that the Supernatural Order is not something added to the Natural Order, like music or painting, to make everyday life more tolerable? It *is* everyday life. The supernatural is real; what we call 'real' is a mere shadow, a passing fancy. Don't you agree, Padre?" "Up to a point," the obviously uncomfortable chaplain replies.[3]

A theologian might quibble with Guy Crouchback's description of the "real world" as "mere shadow," but every influential Catholic thinker in history would have agreed with Guy's basic proposition: that what we call the "supernatural" is, in truth, the most real of real things, and that the supernatural makes itself known to us through the materials of the "real world." In the Catholic imagination, what we call the "real world" is not buttoned down and self-enclosed. The "real world" is a world with windows, doors, and skylights. Into it streams the light of what is really the real world, which is the world of the supernatural: the world of God.

In the Catholic imagination, the extraordinary lies just on

the far side of the ordinary. Through the ordinary things of this world—"outward signs," an old catechism called them—God makes himself and his grace available to us in what Catholics call "sacraments." As Guy Crouchback knew even in his cups, the "Catholic imagination," the Catholic way of looking at things, is a sacramental imagination. Inside that distinctive way of looking at things, what the world often thinks of as ordinary and mundane becomes an experience of the extraordinary and the divine.

That sacramental imagination is the only context in which debates about the shape of the Church's worship and the character of the Church's priesthood make sense.

"Shining from Shook Foil"

The grittiness of this Catholic imagination about the world—this sacramental intuition about the extraordinary revealed in the seemingly ordinary—is memorably captured in Gerard Manley Hopkins's poem "God's Grandeur":

> The world is charged with the grandeur of God.
>   It will flame out, like shining from shook foil;
>   It gathers to a greatness, like the ooze of oil
> Crushed. Why do men then now not reck his rod?
> Generations have trod, have trod, have trod;
>   And all is seared with trade; bleared, smeared with toil;
>   And wears man's smudge and shares man's smell: the soil
> Is bare now, nor can foot feel, being shod.

And for all this, nature is never spent;
  There lives the dearest freshness deep down things;
And though the last lights off the black West went
  Oh, morning, at the brown brink eastward, springs—
Because the Holy Ghost over the bent
  World broods with warm breast and with ah! bright wings.

Catholicism's sacramental view of the world is not pantheism. Pantheism identifies God with the things of the world. In the Catholic sacramental imagination, the world remains the world but the world is not just the world. For real-world things can become vehicles of God's presence, through God's grace. The place where this happens most intensely, most palpably, is in the Church's worship, the liturgy.

The Catholic sacramental imagination and the distinctive experience of worship to which it gives rise have their roots in the Hebrew Bible. In the journey of the people of Israel from slavery to freedom, which is repeated morally and spiritually throughout the Old Testament after the Jewish people's liberation from Egypt, rituals arise. These are not the nature rituals of pagan antiquity, meant to celebrate cosmic cycles or to appease manipulable gods. Israel's rituals—circumcision, the anointing of priests and kings, the sacrifices—are acts that make present once again, through the materials of this world, God's saving deeds for his chosen people. Foremost among these rituals is the Passover celebration. As celebrated by faithful Jews, the Passover is no mere commemoration. Rather, the Passover meal is a ritual that, through such concrete things as bitter herbs, a roast lamb, and a recounting of history, makes present again—"re-presents"—the miraculous experience of the Exodus and Sinai: Israel's passage from slavery to freedom and the covenant of mutual obligation that God seals with his people so that they do not fall back into the habits of slaves.

Jesus makes similar use of material things in his ministry to illustrate the central point of his proclamation—that "the Kingdom of God is in the midst of you" (*Luke* 17.21). Jesus' healings, in which mud and spittle become means to recovering sight, are one example. In his parables, Jesus constantly uses the things of this world—seed, trees, doors, foundations, weeds, yeast, hidden treasures, a fisherman's net—to illustrate aspects of the Kingdom of God, the really real world. That use of material things for making the Kingdom come alive reaches its high point at the Last Supper, a Passover supper. There, Jesus identifies himself with bread and wine, transforming them into his body and blood, so that his disciples and all who come after them may enter into the most intimate communion with God.

In the Catholic sacramental imagination about the world, everything that is, is of consequence. Everything counts. Water, oil, and salt, a lighted candle and a white garment are the vehicles by which newborns and adult converts become sons and daughters of God in baptism. Oil seals Christians with the gift of the Holy Spirit in confirmation; oil brings comfort to the ill and the dying in the sacrament of the sick; oil prepares the hands of priests and bishops for their ministry. Bread and wine, broken and shared, become the body and blood of Christ in the Eucharist. The sacrament of marriage is conferred by husband and wife on each other; the physical consummation of the truth that they are now "one flesh" completes the wedding that began with their vows.

The seven sacraments of the Catholic Church in the strict sense of the term—baptism, confirmation, Holy Eucharist, penance (or the sacrament of reconciliation), holy orders, matrimony, and the anointing of the sick—are seven privileged moments in the Christian life in which God's grace is conferred in a particularly powerful way. The seven sacraments—these seven signs which convey God's life and grace in a singular way, making present what they symbolize—confirm the Catholic sacramental imagination about the world and illustrate how the extraordinary touches us through the ordinary. At the same time, the sacraments are just that, sacraments, because God has structured reality sacramentally. Nothing is mere coincidence or chance. The stuff of this world is like "shining from shook foil," replete with the grandeur of God.

God's Work

Asked to cite the most important text of the Second Vatican Council, theologians might list the *Dogmatic Constitution on the Church* or the *Dogmatic Constitution on Divine Revelation*. Activists would rate the *Pastoral Constitution on the Church in the Modern World* highly, while anyone interested in Church/state issues would give pride of place to the *Declaration on Religious Freedom*. Ask any ordinary, in-the-pew Catholic what the Second Vatican Council did, and the answer is likely to be, "It changed the Mass."

The renewal of the Church's worship was Vatican II's first

order of business, and the changes came rapidly and visibly. The Mass had been celebrated in Latin for centuries. Within five years of the Council, the Mass and all the Church's other liturgical celebrations were in the language of the people and an endless series of debates about translations (especially into English) began. The priest now celebrated Mass facing the people across the altar, and the people, whom liturgy specialists now called "the assembly," took an active role in the service: singing and leading the community's song, making responses to prayers, reading the Scripture lessons, bringing the bread and wine to the altar before their consecration, distributing holy communion, exchanging a sign of peace and fellowship prior to receiving communion. Liturgical chant was largely abandoned, only to be rediscovered a quarter century later by Generation X, which sent a chant CD from a hitherto obscure Spanish monastery to the top of both the pop and classical charts. Hymns became a staple of Catholic worship; and new liturgical music, some of it heavily influenced by the popular music of the time, was written.

The bishops of Vatican II had written that the primary means to the renewal of the Church's liturgy, and thus to the renewal of the entire Church as a vibrant evangelical movement, was to promote the "full, conscious, and active participation" of all those present at the Church's liturgical celebrations.[4] The liturgy was not, in other words, a matter of the priest acting and the congregation mutely observing. Because all those present at Mass were members of "a chosen race, a royal priesthood, a holy nation, a redeemed people" (*1 Peter* 2.9), each had a baptismal "right and obligation" to participate actively in the Church's worship.[5] The bishops also knew that this idea was going to take some getting used to, and urged that Catholics be prepared for active liturgical participation by effective instruction. Some of that undoubtedly took place. It may be wondered, though, just how comprehensive and effective that instruction was.

Though a small minority continues to find these changes difficult to accept, most Catholics have welcomed them enthusiastically, according to the available survey research. It is true that Catholic practice, including attendance at Sunday Mass and reception of the sacrament of penance (still called, by most Catholics, "going to confession"), has declined since Vatican II, in some instances precipitously. It would be a logical fallacy to assume that what happened after the Council always happened because of the Council, however. In the broadest terms, liturgical renewal has been widely accepted, and it is nostalgic to imagine a return to the way things were.

Still, intense and interesting debates about the liturgical reform continue among Catholics of various theological and aesthetic persuasions who are committed to what they call a "reform of the reform." Some scholars are now questioning whether the historical models that underwrote the simplifications of the reformed liturgy were accurate. Very few Catholics with any sense of the majesty of the English language admire the translations currently used at Mass. Ecumenical Councils always produce controversies, and it seems likely that the liturgical controversies generated by Vatican II will continue for decades to come. Those controversies will be constructive rather than destructive—and the liturgy will be more attractive to the curious and the skeptical—if Catholics can manage to agree on one crucial point: that the liturgy is, in the deepest sense, God's work, not ours.

Liturgy, like much else in Catholic life, has been bureaucratized in recent decades. Most parishes have liturgy committees, and in many instances Sunday worship is planned by a committee. There is nothing wrong with this in itself, but it helps contribute to the notion that liturgy is something we make rather than something of God's making in which we participate. That self-conscious sense of creating the liturgy is also reinforced by one of the unanticipated results of having the priest face the people during Mass: the priest-celebrant's personality becomes the dominant factor in the liturgy.

It may seem arcane to suggest that the liturgy is God's work, not ours, since everyone knows that liturgical texts are of human origin and can change. The issue is not the authorship of the Church's prayer books, however, but the nature of worship itself. One way to grasp the liturgy as our participation in God's work is to go back to the Hebrew Bible and reflect on the famous incident in which Moses catches the people of Israel worshiping a golden calf fashioned by his brother, Aaron.

In his book *The Spirit of the Liturgy,* Cardinal Joseph Ratzinger offers an instructive commentary on that dramatic scene from *Exodus.* Even within the Old Testament, the worship of the golden calf is typically presented as an episode of simple idolatry, the worship of false gods. As Psalm 106 has it, "They fashioned a calf at Horeb / and worshiped an image of metal, / exchanging the God who was their glory / for the image of a bull that eats grass." Cardinal Ratzinger suggests that the idolatry here reaches even further.

Aaron, the cardinal writes, doesn't intend to foster a "cult . . . of the false gods of the heathens." And inwardly, Ratzinger argues, the people of Israel "remain completely attached to the same God . . . who led Israel out of Egypt." So what is the problem? Wherein lies Israel's apostasy? First, in the notion that the saving power of the one true God can be properly represented by a golden calf. "The people cannot cope with the invisible, remote, and mysterious God," Cardinal Ratzinger writes. "They want to bring him down into their own world, into what they can see and understand." So they end up worshiping falsely: the worship of the golden calf "is no longer going up to God, but drawing God down into one's own world. He must be there when he is needed, and he must be the kind of God that is needed."

In this false worship, "man is using God, and . . . even if it is not outwardly discernible, he is placing himself above God." Worshiping golden calves, we worship gods made in our own image and likeness, rather than acknowledging our dependence on the God who made us in his divine image and likeness.

Which brings us to the second, subtle apostasy. Worshiping the golden calf, Israel indulges in what Cardinal Ratzinger calls a "self-generated cult." False worship is a feast we give ourselves, a "festival of self-affirmation." Rather than being worship of God, worship "becomes a circle closed in on itself: eating, drinking, and making merry." That is why Moses explodes in anger when he discovers the Israelite camp in revelry: "The dance around the golden calf is . . . self-seeking worship. It is a kind of banal self-gratification. Ultimately, it is no longer concerned with God but with giving oneself a nice little alternative world, manufactured from one's own resources."[6]

Are Catholics today immune to this temptation? Monsignor M. Francis Mannion, former rector of Salt Lake City's Cathedral of the Madeleine and now director of the Liturgical Institute at Chicago's University of St. Mary of the Lake, thinks not. Monsignor Mannion, a leader in the "reform of the reform," argues that a "fundamental problem facing the Mass today is the cultural corruption of its celebration through the importation of conceptions and practices of consumerism, entertainment, and psychotherapy." Rather than letting "the richness and depth of the rites speak for themselves," Mannion suggests, "the eucharistic liturgy is often buried by cultural overlays which deprive the Church's central sacrament of its power."[7]

When the Mass becomes entertainment, therapy, or therapeutic entertainment, it is not what it is meant to be. When the priest-celebrant, or the congregation, or both the celebrant and the congregation imagine themselves to be the real point of reference for the liturgy, the liturgy is not what it is meant to be. We do not worship God because it makes us feel better, or good, or entertained. We worship God because God is to be worshiped. According to ancient Catholic teaching reiterated by Vatican II, the privilege of Catholic worship is that it is a participation in "the heavenly liturgy which is celebrated in the Holy City of Jerusalem toward which we journey as pilgrims, where Christ is sitting at the right hand of God, minister of the holies and of the true tabernacle."[8] To participate in the Mass here is not to look down or to look around, but to look up: it is to join with the angels and saints who praise God throughout eternity.

The real point of reference for the liturgy is God the Holy

Trinity: Christ leads us, through the power of the Spirit, into authentic worship of the Father. Like true love, true worship doesn't mean looking into each other's eyes. It means looking together at the God who is Love.

Understanding that is the beginning of the reform of liturgical reform in the Catholic Church.

The Priest as Icon

Cardinal Francis George of Chicago is frequently asked why the Church doesn't ordain women to the ministerial priesthood. A former teacher and a man of constant conversation, the cardinal usually responds, "You tell me what you think a priest is and we'll take it from there." The answer the cardinal then gets is almost always a functional one: a priest is someone who does certain things. And if that is what priests are, then it seems unfair, even unjust, to ordain only men to the priesthood.

Would the entire question look different if it were viewed through the prism of the sacramental imagination? Suppose a Catholic priest is not a set of functions, but an *icon*?

The idea that the priesthood is essentially functional is an unhappy by-product of centuries of legalization and bureaucratization in the Catholic Church, the net result of which was a kind of clerical caste system. The Second Vatican Council and Pope John Paul II have tried to remedy this deformation. The Council reminded the Church that there is one high priest, Jesus Christ, in whose unique priesthood every Christian shares by baptism. The ordained, ministerial priesthood is not a set of functions within this "common priesthood" of all the baptized. Nor does the ordained priest represent the priestly community made up of all Christians the way a member of Congress represents a district—the priest does not "stand in" for the community. In the Catholic view of things, the ordained priest is an icon of Christ the high priest. The ordained priest is an ordinary man who, by the grace of holy orders, becomes an extraordinary symbol—an extraordinary "re-presentation"—of Christ's priestly presence to his people.

The ordained priesthood exists not as a caste for its own sake, but for the service of the common priesthood of all the people of God. That is one reason why the Catholic Church in the West values celibacy so highly: celibacy chosen for the sake of the Kingdom of God, in which all will live in a communion of perfect giving and receptivity, is a powerful sign to the entire Church of every Christian's destiny (see *Matthew* 19.12). The ordained priest, as an icon of Christ the Priest, lifts up and ennobles the common priesthood of all God's people, enabling the community to worship in truth, speak the truth, and serve in truth. John Paul II has insisted time and again that the ministerial priesthood is not a career and it is not about power. It is about service. "The New Testament witness and the constant tradition of the Church," the Pope writes, "remind us that the ministerial priesthood cannot be understood in sociological or political categories, as a matter of exercising 'power' within the community. The priesthood of Holy Orders must be understood theologically, as one form of service in and for the Church."[9]

The priesthood, in the Catholic view of things, cannot be

grasped in terms of "rights," and the issue of the possible ordination of women to the priesthood cannot be understood as a question of justice. Strictly speaking, no one has a "right" to be a priest, and no man's claim to a priestly vocation is ever taken by the Church at face value. Priestly vocations are tested through a lengthy period of preparation. The Church calls men to the priesthood. No one, from the Pope to the humblest rural pastor, has called himself to be a priest as a matter of his own empowerment.

Nor can we understand justice in the Church by strict comparison to justice in society. The personal equality of all the people of the Church by reason of their being created in the image of God, and their spiritual equality because of their baptism, exists alongside a necessary difference, or inequality, of spiritual gifts. Those differences, or inequalities, are of God's doing, and we should not wish it to be otherwise. Unless some were given the gift of prophetic insight, how would the rest of us be challenged to see things as they really are? Unless others were given the gift of spiritual direction, who would the rest of us look to for guidance on our pilgrimage through life? The equality of all before the law is a bedrock principle of a just civil society. The variety of gifts given by the same Holy Spirit, the different kinds of service rendered to the same Lord, and the many works in which God is working (*1 Corinthians* 12.4–6)—these are the bedrock reality of the Church, which is a communion of believers, not a nation-state.[10]

Then there is what we might call the "body language" of the priesthood. In the Catholic sacramental imagination, maleness and femaleness are neither accidents of evolutionary biology nor cultural constructs, but icons pointing to deep truths about the nature of reality and the nature of God. The equality of men and women, made in the image of God and redeemed by Christ, does not mean that men and women are interchangeable as icons of God's presence to the world. This insistence on taking seriously our sexual embodiedness, our distinctive maleness and femaleness, is at the root of the Church's sexual ethic. It is also involved in the question of the priesthood.

According to the ancient tradition of the Church, going back to St. Paul and the first generation of Christian believers, Christ's relationship to the Church is spousal, or nuptial: Christ loves the Church as a husband loves a wife (*Ephesians* 5.25). That spousal giving in love is most thoroughly re-presented in the Eucharist, at Mass, when the priest, acting in the person of Christ and as an icon of Christ, makes Christ's gift of himself present through the consecration of the bread and wine that become Christ's body and blood. For Christian communities in which the Lord's Supper is a memorial meal, a sharing of table fellowship, the issue of women as ordained ministers is no issue, or simply a question of custom, because the ministry is functional, not sacramental. That is not the Catholic understanding of the Eucharist or the ordained ministry. The iconography of Christ's spousal gift of self to his Church, most intensely embodied in his sacramental giving of himself in the Eucharist, requires, in the Catholic view of things, a priest who can iconographically re-present Christ in his male donation of himself to his bride, the Church.

None of this is easy to engage, much less grasp, in a culture that treats sexual differentiation as accidental, not sacramental—a unisex culture, so to speak. Still, the truth of the matter is that the Catholic tradition of ordaining only men to the priesthood is an expression of the Catholic sacramental imagination. It is not a matter of misogyny. It is not a question of rights. It is not a question of power. It is a question of sacramentality. The extraordinary that lies just on the far side of the ordinary is made present through the things of this world, weak and inadequate as they may be—as weak and inadequate as those men called to the priesthood would say they undoubtedly are. But God's ways, as the prophet Isaiah reminded God's people, are not ours (*Isaiah* 55.8). That is abundantly true of the sacramental imagination.

Prayer and God's Thirst for Us

Finally, in this context, a word about prayer.

If Christianity is God in search of us, then Christian prayer must somehow reflect that truth. The *Catechism of the Catholic Church* chooses the story of Christ and the Samaritan woman to illustrate that point. In the Gospel story (*John* 4.4–26), Jesus is sitting by Jacob's well in the heat of the afternoon when a Samaritan woman comes to draw water from the well. "Give me a drink," Jesus asks the woman, who is surprised that a Jew would speak to a Samaritan. For the *Catechism,* Christ's question and the woman's surprise illuminate the surprising character of prayer: "The wonder of prayer is revealed beside the well where we come seeking water; there, Christ comes to meet every human being. It is he who first seeks us and asks us for a drink. Jesus thirsts; his asking arises from the depths of God's desire for us. Whether we realize it or not, prayer is the encounter of God's thirst with ours. God thirsts that we may thirst for him."[11]

Guy Crouchback had a similar insight in the third volume of Evelyn Waugh's *Sword of Honour* trilogy. At his father's funeral Mass, Captain Crouchback meditates on his own most serious sin—the spiritual sloth that theologians call "acedia":

> For many years now the direction in the *Garden of the Soul,* "Put yourself in the presence of God," had for Guy come to mean a mere act of respect, like the signing of the Visitors' Book at an Embassy or Government House. He reported for duty saying to God: "I don't ask anything from you. I am here if you want me. I don't suppose I can be of any use, but if there is anything I can do, let me know," and left it at that.
>
> "I don't ask anything from you": that was the deadly core of his apathy, his father had tried to tell him, was now telling him. That emptiness had been with him for years now even in his days of enthusiasm and activity with the Halberdiers. Enthusiasm and activity were not enough. God required more than that. He had commanded all men to *ask.*[12]

Prayer, according to an old Catholic formula, is "the lifting up of our minds and hearts to God." Primarily, the Scriptures would insist, prayer is a matter of our heart. More than a thousand times, the Hebrew Bible and the New Testament refer to the "heart," that "place to which I withdraw," that sanctuary of my inmost self, as the place from which prayer comes.[13] This suggests that although the sacramental imagination can be analyzed intellectually, it is, in the final analysis, a matter of the heart: a matter of apprehension rather than comprehension, a knowing that is akin to loving.

To pray is a way of experiencing and sharing in love: the love that is the inner life of God, Father, Son, and Holy Spirit.

5

How Should We Live?

The Moral Life and the Laws That Liberate

From the outside, the Catholic Church can seem like an irascible, arbitrary nanny, constantly dunning her charges with impossible proscriptions. "Don't" is the keyword that gets you to the Catholic moral Web site, from an outsider's view of things. It is not a very attractive image, and it impedes a serious encounter with one of the world's most experienced moral teachers. That is a loss for everyone.

On the other hand, there is a certain challenging truth here. The Catholic Church's resolute refusal to abandon certain classic moral convictions has created controversies beyond numbering. Our culture will accept a kind of moral vocabulary, but only if it's a vocabulary of preference: "I *wish* you'd do this" or "I'd *prefer* that you don't do that." Any alternative vocabulary—for example, "You really *ought* to do this" or

"You really *shouldn't* do that"—is easily labeled authoritarian and dismissed as an encroachment on our freedom.

That has been a widespread response to Catholic moral teaching during the past thirty years or so. The teaching is simply rejected as institutional authoritarianism. The convictions about the dynamics of human life and happiness that are the foundation of the teaching are rarely explored.

There is another piece of the truth in that negative image of the Catholic Church as a moral teacher. For centuries, Catholic moral teaching was typically presented as a string of prohibitions. But this "prohibition-first" approach to morality was a serious distortion of the classic Catholic concept of the moral life. In the prohibition-first view, morality is a contest of wills between my will and God's will. God's will is stronger, and so the meeting point between my will and God's is moral obligation. The crucial moral question is "How far can I go before I run into an obligation being imposed by that stronger will?" The moral life conceived as a laundry list of prohibitions easily follows.

"How far can I go?" was not the question the rich young man asked Jesus, in the gospel story that Pope John Paul II proposes as the paradigm of the moral life. His was a different question: "Teacher, what good must I do to have eternal life?" (*Matthew* 19.16). The rich young man didn't ask what he shouldn't do; he asked what good he ought to do. Moreover, the point of doing good was not to assert his autonomy, exercise his free will, or feel good about himself. The point was "to have eternal life."

Here is a microcosm of the moral life as Catholicism once

understood it, and as the Catholic Church is beginning to understand it again at the beginning of the third millennium: the moral life is fundamentally a question of *goodness,* of becoming a good person. The point of being a good person is that goodness equips us to enjoy eternal life. It takes a certain kind of person to be able to enjoy God's life, with God, forever. We have to grow into the kind of people who can do that. That growth takes place through our freedom. The prescriptions and proscriptions of the moral law are boundaries for exercising our freedom. They help us to choose the good freely, and that is how we develop into the kind of people who can live with God forever.

Much of the debate about Catholic moral teaching is still locked into the old, rule-bound paradigm. Arguments devolve into fruitless and often nasty debates between defenders of strict rules and advocates of lax rules. One sets the bar high; the other tries to lower it. Neither talks very much about goodness and happiness. Both tend to present "the rules" as an infringement on freedom, because they imagine that freedom is willfulness. One defends restrictions on freedom, while the other chafes at what it agrees are restrictions. Neither asks whether freedom might be something different—whether freedom might not have something to do with the happiness of becoming the kind of person who freely chooses what is good.

The way out of this box—the way to get the rules of the moral life into the right focus—is to go back to the story of Jesus and the rich young man. As it's often presented in sermons, the climax of the story is a warning against materialism and avarice: the rich young man turns away because "he had great possessions" and couldn't bear to part with them. If we read further in Matthew's Gospel, the real challenge to the rich young man was not simply to give up his possessions, but to give himself: "If you would be perfect, go, sell what you possess and give it to the poor, and you will have treasure in heaven; and come, follow me" (*Matthew* 19.21). Give yourself away, Jesus asks. Make yourself, not just your possessions, into a gift.

That is the fundamental challenge of the moral life in classic Catholic terms: the challenge to make ourselves a gift to others. Everything else—including rules and laws, prescriptions and proscriptions—revolves around that. Giving ourselves equips us to be the kind of people who can live with God, a Trinity of self-giving Persons, forever.

The moral life is not something added on to real life from the outside. The moral life is life as lived by human beings. Because our lives are inescapably moral lives, they have an inherently dramatic structure. We live in the gap between the person we are today and the person we ought to be. According to Jesus in the gospel story of the rich young man, we close that gap by growing, under grace, in the capacity to dispose of ourselves freely in self-giving love.

Morality is not limited to commands and duties, although morality involves commands and duties. Viewed from inside, morality is about happiness and the virtues that make for happiness. Love is the center of the moral life for Catholics—love that disposes of itself as gift, making us the kind of givers who can live for eternity with radically self-giving Love.

Fitness for Beatitude

If the point of the moral life is to prepare us to become the kind of people who can live with God forever, then the first place we should look for clues to a specifically Christian morality is the Sermon on the Mount, which one contemporary Catholic moral theologian calls a "charter of the Christian life." And the first place we should look in the Sermon on the Mount is the Beatitudes.[1] For "beatitude," eternal happiness, is what living with God means.

The Beatitudes (*Matthew* 5.3–12) are sometimes taken to be a preamble to the real meat of the Sermon on the Mount, in which Jesus challenges his listeners to be salt and light for the world, to live in mercy beyond the strict demands of justice, and to call God "our Father" in prayer. St. Augustine teaches us, though, that the Beatitudes are the keystone of Christ's entire discourse on human happiness. "We all want to live happily," Augustine writes; "in the whole human race there is no one who does not assent to this proposition." The Beatitudes are Christ's response to the deeply felt human yearning for happiness.

Far from being a matter of psychology or brain chemistry, that desire for happiness is of divine origin, according to the *Catechism of the Catholic Church:* "God has placed it in the human heart in order to draw man to the One who alone can fulfill it."[2] The Beatitudes—with their promise of eternal happiness for the poor in spirit, the mourners, the meek, those who hunger and thirst for righteousness, the merciful, the peacemakers, and the persecuted—teach us that our acts have the most profound consequences, because what we do makes us into the kind of people we are. And what we are determines what we can be: for God calls into the happiness of his own beatitude all those who have made themselves into a gift through living the Beatitudes.

The Beatitudes—and the eternal happiness to which they point—set the context for the Christian moral life. As the *Catechism* puts it, "The beatitude we are promised confronts us with decisive moral choices. It invites us to purify our hearts of bad instincts and to seek the love of God above all else. It teaches us that true happiness is not found in riches or well-being, in human fame or power, or in any human achievement . . . but in God alone, the source of every good and of all love."[3] The beatitude of heaven, of life with God, sets standards for discerning what is good in life in this world. The moral life is not a set of arbitrary rules that can be changed like the rules of basketball or baseball. There is a built-in quality to the moral law: rules for living emerge from inside the human heart and its yearning for happiness with God.

Freedom for Excellence

Reimagining the moral life through the prism of the Beatitudes takes us from rules to virtues: from a *rule*-centered idea of morality to a *virtue*-centered idea of morality. The basic question changes from "How far can I go?" to "What should I do to become a good person?" In discovering answers to that far more profound question, rules will come into focus, but those rules are not arbitrary impositions from outside the human condition. The rules emerge from the very dynamics of the human quest for happiness. They are, so to speak, built into the quest itself.

All of which leads to an idea of freedom very different from the one we often encounter in our culture.

Freedom today is typically understood as willfulness: doing what we like, doing it "my way." On this understanding, freedom is a faculty of choice, and choice is everything. Freedom has no goal other than what I choose in any given circumstance. Because freedom is simply choice, freedom can attach itself to anything as long as no one else gets hurt in the process. Here, the suggestion that certain choices are simply incompatible with our dignity as human beings, with our freedom, is an arbitrary and unacceptable infringement on freedom. "I did it my way" describes the highest value in the moral life.

The great nineteenth-century English historian of freedom, Lord Acton, had a dramatically different point of view. Freedom, Acton insisted, is not the power to do whatever we like. Instead, freedom is having the right to do what we ought. Freedom and goodness are intimately, inextricably related.

We can begin to get an idea of what Acton meant, and how it leads us to a richer, more human concept of freedom, by thinking about two ways in which we develop as human beings: playing a musical instrument and learning a new language. Learning to play the piano can be a tedious business, involving disciplined exercises by which we train our minds and our fingers. At the beginning, every piano student experiences those exercises as a burden, a constraint. After a while, though, what we once experienced as constraining seems liberating. Mastering those exercises has equipped me to play anything I want, including the most difficult compositions. What seemed like drudgery has even equipped me to create new music on my own.

Anyone, of course, is free to pound away on a piano, making haphazard noise, but as an eminent moral theologian, Father Servais Pinckaers, notes, "This is a rudimentary, savage sort of freedom," which "cloaks an incapacity to play even the simplest pieces accurately and well." Those who have done their exercises have really mastered the art of playing the piano, and by becoming artists they have acquired a new freedom. This deeper, richer, more human freedom is a matter of gradually acquiring the capacity to do what we choose with perfection.

Learning a new language is similar. Hearing and speaking are the best way to learn a language. At some point in the process, though, we have to learn the basic rules of grammar and we have to develop a vocabulary, which is another set of rules. The rules make language possible. Speech without rules is just noise. Speech within rules is truly human: it's language, communication, a way of meeting and engaging others. Here, too, Father Pinckaers suggests, is a "new kind of freedom." We are living within a set of rules, but we are free to choose the words we like to make our sentences. It is not the freedom to make mistakes; it is the freedom to avoid mistakes without thinking about it. It's the habit, the virtue, of speaking properly and well.

Father Pinckaers calls this "freedom for excellence," and it stands in sharp contrast to freedom as my way, or freedom as willfulness.[4] Doing it my way is like banging on the piano or speaking gibberish. Doing things the right way is doing things the human way, the truly free way. We are made for freedom,

Father Pinckaers suggests. We are made for a freedom that is lived by developing the habits of mind and heart—the virtues—that enable us to satisfy our natural attraction to happiness, our natural disposition toward the good. Every human being, Pinckaers writes, has "basic moral inclinations" and a "primal moral sense" that "no corruption . . . can completely destroy." To grow in the moral life is to develop our moral habits so that we know and do what is good almost as a matter of instinct. That is how we grow into the kind of people who can live with God, who is all goodness.

We need to be educated in freedom. In that education we learn to be attracted to what is truly good, beautiful, and conducive to our happiness. The morality of Christian freedom is a morality of attraction, not simply of obligation. "One becomes free only by becoming better," according to an old Catholic maxim. We become better by developing that interior voice, that conscience, by which we are attracted to the good and the beautiful—to what is truly worthy of our love and commitment.[5]

THE LAW THAT LIBERATES

In the moral life, as in learning to play the piano or learning a language, rules bind and free at the same time. During his pilgrimage to Mt. Sinai during the jubilee year of 2000, Pope John Paul II suggested that this is the way we should think about the Ten Commandments.

God's gift of the Ten Commandments on Mt. Sinai is intimately connected to God's liberation of the people of Israel from their slavery in Egypt. According to the Hebrew Bible, the Jewish people had been in bondage for 430 years when Moses led them out of slavery into freedom. In more than four hundred years a people can pick up a lot of habits, including bad habits. As their complaints against God and Moses in the desert after the Exodus made clear, the people of Israel retained many of the habits of slaves even after they had left the bondage of Egypt. At certain points in their journey those habits, and the attitudes they reinforced, were so overwhelming that the people asked to be returned to slavery: "Why did we come forth out of Egypt?" (*Numbers* 11.20).

The Ten Commandments were a moral code given to the people of Israel to keep them from falling back into the habits of slaves. God intended Israel's liberation to be comprehensive: it was a liberation from the hard hand of the Egyptian taskmasters and a liberation from the habits of mind and heart by which a people had become accustomed to being slaves. If the people of Israel were to continue to live as free people, they had to rid themselves of the habits of slaves and learn the habits of free men and women. They had to learn the habits, the virtues, of freedom.

That is what the Ten Commandments are for. The Ten Commandments are an elementary school of freedom—freedom lived for goodness and happiness, freedom lived according to laws that liberate. These are the basics. Without them, neither the moral life nor any sort of genuine freedom is possible.

The Ten Commandments are not a capricious set of injunctions, but basic moral rules that emerge from taking the human thirst for goodness and the human desire for happiness seriously. When he made his Mt. Sinai pilgrimage during the

Great Jubilee of 2000, Pope John Paul II underscored the truth that the Ten Commandments were not the peremptory moral decrees of some otherworldly divinity but a liberating code intended to keep all of us from falling into the habits of slaves. The "encounter of God and Moses on this mountain enshrines at the heart of our religion *the mystery of liberating obedience,*" the Pope said. "The Ten Commandments are not the arbitrary imposition of a tyrannical Lord. They were written in stone; but before that, they were written on the human heart as the universal moral law. . . . They save man from the destructive force of egoism, hatred, and falsehood. They point out the false gods that draw him into slavery: the love of self to the exclusion of God, the greed for power and pleasure that . . . degrades our human dignity and that of our neighbor." The liberation promised by these rules that bind and free at the same time is an eternal liberation: "If we turn from . . . false idols and follow the God who sets his people free and remains always with them, then we shall emerge like Moses, after forty days on the mountain, 'shining with glory,' ablaze with the light of God!"

For the Christian, John Paul concluded, the Ten Commandments are heard and lived through our encounter with Jesus Christ. Christ delivers us into true freedom. Christ, too, binds and frees at the same time. His is a binding that leads to the fullness of liberation. Those who are bound to Christ and bound by Christ know that they are bound "*not externally,* by a multitude of prescriptions, *but internally,* by the love which has taken hold in the deepest recesses of [the] heart." Thus "the Ten Commandments are the law of freedom . . . *the freedom to love, to choose what is good in every situation.*" When God revealed himself and his law to Moses, he revealed to human beings the truth about the human condition. The Ten Commandments *"stand at the very heart of the truth about man and his destiny."*[6] To be faithful to the Ten Commandments, to be faithful to the God who wrote them in our hearts and on the tablets of the law, "is being faithful to ourselves, to our true nature, and to our deepest and irrepressible aspirations."[7]

No one really wants to be a slave—which is life at the whim of an arbitrary outside authority. However much we dislike the idea of slavery, though, we all have inclinations that can enslave us. That is why there are many slaves in the world today, even after slavery has been legally abolished.

To live freely means to rid ourselves of the habits of slaves, just as the people of Israel were called to do at Mt. Sinai. To worship rightly, to honor parents and the sanctity of life, to deal honestly and justly with others—these are the virtues of freedom, the habits of free men and women. That is why God enjoined them in the Ten Commandments—to bind us in order to liberate us for goodness and for love.

Conscience and the Primacy of Truth

Getting rid of the habits of slaves is no easy business. Everyone fails from time to time; some fail often. That failure to live freedom excellently is what the Catholic Church means by sin. Sin, the *Catechism of the Catholic Church* teaches, is an "abuse of freedom." It is a slavish habit that weakens our capacity to love others and to love God.[8] When we indulge those bad habits we come to see God as a limitation on our freedom, rather than as the source and fulfillment of that freedom.[9] Which brings us to Satan, and conscience.

Satan, G. K. Chesterton famously said, "fell by the force of gravity"—his own.[10] Satan took himself so seriously that he became incapable of taking anything else seriously, including God. Satan's freedom became a terrible weight rather than a liberating openness.

The temptation to take ourselves with ultimate seriousness often expresses itself in claims about the "primacy of conscience." Discussions of conscience frequently invoke the example of Thomas More, the sixteenth-century English statesman and onetime lord chancellor of England who died rather than bend to the will of King Henry VIII. Since most of the world today knows Thomas More from Robert Bolt's play and film *A Man for All Seasons,* a critical look at that fine drama helps sort out the truth about More and the truth about conscience.

In a preface to his play, Bolt writes that the world's greatest need is for "a sense of selfhood without resort to magic." More was a hero for Bolt because

> Thomas More . . . [was] a man with an adamantine sense of his own self. He knew where he began and left off, what area of himself he could yield to the encroachments of his enemies, and what to the encroachments of those he loved. . . . Since he was a clever man and a great lawyer he was able to retire from those areas in wonderfully good order, but at length he was asked to retreat from that final

> area where he located his self. And there this supple, humorous, unassuming and sophisticated person set like metal, was overtaken by an absolutely primitive rigor, and could no more be budged than a cliff.[11]

This is splendid, even gripping, writing. But it isn't what Thomas More was about.

A Man for All Seasons was first performed in the early 1960s, when existentialism was in intellectual fashion. Bolt's More is something of an existentialist hero, dying a martyr's death because truckling to King Henry VIII would have violated his sense of "self." To put it in moral terms, More was a martyr for conscience. Thus, in one of the great exchanges in a play filled with brilliant repartee, More's friend the Duke of Norfolk asks why Sir Thomas can't accede to the king's demands as so many others among the great and good had already done: "You know these men! Can't you do what I did, and come with us, for fellowship?" To which More, moved by his friend's concern, replies, "And when we stand before God, and you are sent to Paradise for doing according to your conscience, and I am damned for not doing according to mine, will you come with me, for fellowship?"[12]

It's a beautiful passage, but it misses the crucial point. Thomas More did not die for the "primacy of conscience," if by that we mean the primacy of his autonomous and willful "self." More died for Christian truth. As John Paul II wrote his apostolic letter naming St. Thomas More the patron of politicians and statesmen during the Great Jubilee of 2000, More's "passion for truth . . . enlightened his conscience" and taught him the truths for which he died: "that man cannot be sundered from God, nor politics from morality."[13] More's conscience was not formed privately, by his "self," and it was not ultimately answerable to his "self." Rather, for More, as for John Paul II in the encyclical *Veritatis Splendor* [The Splendor of Truth], conscience is "the witness of God himself, whose voice and judgment penetrate the depths of man's soul."[14]

In doing so, God calls us beyond rational calculation into the realm of freedom, which is the realm of love. *A Man for All Seasons* captures this summons in a wrenching last meeting between More and his family, who have been sent to the Tower of London to persuade him to submit to the king's will. There, after arguing with her father, More's beloved daughter, Meg, finally cries out, "Haven't you done as much as God can reasonably *want*?" To which More, haltingly, replies, "Well . . . finally . . . it isn't a matter of reason; finally it's a matter of love."[15]

Truth is beautiful. Truth is lovable. Moral truth binds and frees at the same time. To be seized by the power of truth is to be seized not by mere rationality, but by the Truth who is Love. According to Bolt, More "found something in himself without which life was valueless and when that was denied him was able to grasp his death."[16] That "something" was the truth of God in Christ.

Thomas More, standing on the brink of eternity, the headsman beside him, took his stand on the primacy of truth as his conscience had been formed by that truth. He did not die to defend his "self." He died for love, and Christian love is self-giving, not self-asserting.

But What About Compassion?

Shortly before Cardinal James A. Hickey retired in January 2000, the *Washington Post* ran a front-page story on his twenty-year stewardship of the Archdiocese of Washington. The article stressed that Cardinal Hickey had been a defender of Catholic moral teaching and a man of broad human sympathy and concern for others. Somehow, though, the reporter thought these qualities were in tension, even contradiction. As she wrote at one point, "Yet when doctrine was set aside, Hickey was unflinching in his compassion for those afflicted with AIDS."[17] A world of confusion was captured in those six words, "Yet when doctrine was set aside . . ." The fact, of course, is that Cardinal Hickey's compassion for those suffering from AIDS was part and parcel of his commitment to Catholic doctrine. He was compassionate because he was committed to the Church's teaching, not in spite of that commitment.

The *Post*'s story was, however, consistent with the conventional story line, which divides Catholicism into politically defined camps, the liberals moved by compassion and the conservatives fixated on moral doctrine. That characterization fails here, as it does in so many other instances, because it can't come to grips with the fact that the Gospel the Catholic Church teaches is a matter of truth, not a matter of liberalism or conservatism. Christians are a people who have been taught by Christ, in Scripture and the living tradition of the Church, the truth about the human condition—that we come from God and are destined for God. That truth, or rule of faith, yields a rule of life: not in the sense of an infinite series of do's and don'ts, but in the sense of a given, changeless standard that measures us and the degree to which we have been faithful to what we have been taught by God's grace. That standard is Christ, in whose life, death, and resurrection we see the true measure of our humanity and its glorious destiny.

There is nothing liberal or conservative about the Catholic Church insisting, calmly and firmly, that she is formed by a rule of faith that is expressed in a rule of life. That rule is no obstacle to compassion. In fact, it is the very condition for the possibility of true compassion. "Compassion," in its Latin root, means "suffering with." If anything goes—if there is no rule of life by which we are liberated, if there is no struggle for virtue and growth into goodness—what is the suffering to be shared and commonly borne?[18]

In a 1993 discussion in Rome of John Paul II's encyclical *Veritatis Splendor,* an influential moral theologian and critic of the Pope's letter argued that to love was "to affirm the other as he understands himself to be." Another theologian replied, "And if he is mistaken in his understanding? What are my obligations in love to him then?" There was no reply.

There couldn't be. "Affirm others as they understand themselves to be" is not a Catholic tenet. It's a tenet of the therapeutic society, in which there is neither rule of faith nor rule of life. To empty the Gospel of its power to set a rule of life is not compassion, and it does not lead to anyone's healing. Moral doctrine—the rule of life that embodies the rule of faith, which is Christ—makes real compassion possible.

A Word About Confession

Why has the Catholic Church laid such emphasis on individual confession over the centuries? Why does Pope John Paul II insist that Catholics have a right to private, auricular confession? Why has confession been, traditionally, such an important part of the spiritual life of the Catholic Church and of Catholic thinking about the moral life?

The Catholic practice of confession to a priest has always puzzled non-Catholic Christians, who wonder why personal confession of sins to the living, risen Christ isn't sufficient. Nonbelievers will wonder whether it's appropriate to unburden oneself of one's most intimate secrets to someone who might well be a stranger. Judging from the precipitous decline in Catholic reception of the sacrament of penance in recent decades, confession now seems to be a mystery to many Catholics, too. Immersed in a self-consciously therapeutic culture, too many Catholics have abandoned a practice that anticipated today's obsession with counseling by centuries. Hundreds of years before therapists discovered that naming our problems was essential to dealing with and resolving them, good confessors knew that—and so did serious penitents. What happened?

Thinking about confession in a dramatic context rather than a legal one may help explain the wisdom of the classic practice. Every Christian life, as we have seen, has the interior structure of a drama. Each Christian life, including the lives of saints, is lived in the gap between the person I am and the person I ought to be. Life within that gap has an inherent dramatic tension to it, and there is no drama without dialogue.

Individual confession is one way the Church creates the opportunity within the drama of the Christian life for that dialogue to unfold in a deeply personal way. That is why going to confession ought not be a matter of simply rattling off a list of transgressions, receiving thirty seconds of counsel, and then being dismissed with a modest penance. Confession within the drama of the Christian life is best understood as a genuine conversation between confessor and penitent.

In that conversation, the penitent reviews the unique circumstances of his or her personal drama with the aid of a fellow Christian. That fellow Christian, a priest acting in the person of Christ, helps the penitent to name the dramatic tension in which he or she is living, to identify the Gospel norms that bear on life within that tension, and to cooperate with God's grace in closing the gap between the person I am and the person I ought to be. Although the sacrament of penance has its legal aspects (because the moral life involves moral laws), the confessional is not primarily a tribunal. It is a place for spiritual discernment, for wise counsel, for a conversation about growing in the virtues. It is a place for experiencing with one's senses the forgiveness of Christ and, through that experience, being empowered to change and grow into the person one ought to be.

Private, individual confession, in which the penitent learns to name the dramatic tension in which he or she is living, is a privileged way to enter more fully into the unique drama of one's Catholic life. The Church's teaching on the priority of individual, private, auricular confession is not a mulish insistence on maintaining a venerable practice just because of its age. It is a defense of the drama of the Christian life, and of the individual Christian's right to be accompanied in that drama by a fellow believer, authorized by Christ and the Church to forgive sins, to reconcile the penitent to God and to the Christian community in Christ's name and by Christ's power.

The reduction of the sacrament of penance to a kind of spiritual mass-production line, as happened too often in the Catholic past, drained confession of its inherent drama. So do moral theologies that teach the relative indifference or inconsequence of particular acts in judging how Catholics are living the Gospel. Recovering a sense of the drama of the moral life, and rediscovering confession as a privileged example of the dialogue in the drama, are antidotes to these ways of diluting Catholic life.

6

How Should We Love?

Celebrating the Gift of Sex

The judgment that the Catholic Church is both prudish and sex-obsessed is deeply entrenched in the Western world today. Catholics and non-Catholics alike believe it. The mass media assumes it. It's simply the way things are, to hundreds of millions of people.

But it's not the way things really are.

Deconstructing the myth of Catholic prudishness and engaging the Catholic sexual ethic for what it really is—namely, an affirmation of the gift of sexuality—means recognizing that the Church itself contributed to the myth's formation. In its first centuries, Christianity decisively rejected the Manichaean heresy, which held that the world was inherently polluted, and took a theologically grounded stand against the claim that sexual love was intrinsically evil. The Church taught that to deprecate sexuality was to deny the great biblical truth contained in *Genesis* 1.31: "God saw everything that he had made, and behold, it was very good." Unfortunately, that principled affirmation of sexual love as one of the goods of God's creation frequently got lost over the centuries in a brier patch of theoretical confusions and legal entanglements.

Catholicism taught that marriage was a vocation, included marriage among the seven sacraments, and insisted that the couple, expressing their love through consent and sexual intimacy, were the ministers of the sacrament of matrimony. Yet for centuries the Church also taught a theory of the "ends," or purposes, of marriage that too often turned into a denigration of sexual love. According to this theory, the "primary end" of marriage, and of sex, was the procreation and education of children. The sexual deepening of married love and the sexual contribution to the communion of husband and wife were relegated to what the old theory called marriage's "secondary ends," which were rather primly described as "mutual consolation of the spouses" and "a remedy for concupiscence." Then there was the Church's marriage law, which dealt with marriage on the analogy of a contract. By adopting a rather depersonalized view of sexuality, it, too, contributed to the widespread notion that for the Catholic Church, sexuality was far more a matter of legal prohibitions than of love.

The Catholic Church never officially taught that sexual love within the bond of marriage was inherently and intrinsically darkened by sin. To the contrary, the old marriage ritual included an instruction to the newlyweds in which they were told that "no greater blessing can come to your married life than pure, conjugal love, loyal and true to the end." But the denigration of sexual love is what many people, including many Catholics, learned from the Catholic Church.

The Church was thus in a very weak position to meet the challenge of the sexual revolution when it broke out into mainstream Western culture in the 1960s. Add to that the antiauthoritarian climate of that decade and one can see why the reaffirmation of the Church's traditional rejection of chemical and mechanical means of contraception in 1968 was either ignored or summarily dismissed as mindless priggishness. To many the Catholic Church's rejection of "the pill" and the "liberated" approach to sexuality the pill made possible seemed all too reminiscent of the Church's rejection of Galileo and the Church's insistence on a geocentric concept of the universe, long after that position became scientifically untenable.

Two generations into the sexual revolution, new questions are being asked. Are the prime beneficiaries of the sexual revolution predatory and irresponsible men, who can now, without serious consequences, indulge the ancient male tendency to treat women as pleasure objects? Has the ubiquity of sexual innuendo in our culture cheapened what the sexual revolution claimed to ennoble? Did the sexual revolution undercut the commitments that make for stable marriages? What do high divorce rates mean for a generation of broken families and for society? Does the high incidence of sexually transmitted disease, and ultimately the AIDS crisis, tell us something disturbing about a culture that treats sex as another contact sport? Is an approach to sexuality that seems to freeze many people into perpetual adolescence really liberating?

Freed from the Manichaean shadow that has dogged it for

centuries, the Catholic sexual ethic can help fulfill the promise of a sexuality liberated from prudery and liberated for love. That has been one of the pastoral priorities of Pope John Paul II since he was a young priest in Poland in the 1950s. Often dismissed as impossibly old hat in matters sexual, John Paul II is in fact a celebrant of sexual love who has been saying to the sexual revolution for four decades, "Human sexuality is greater than you think." Some would argue that the Pope has too high a view of sexual love. Whether that is true or not is a judgment that should be deferred until one explores what the Pope actually has to say on the subject.

What Sex Teaches Us About Ourselves

Father Karol Wojtyła, whom the world would know after October 1978 as Pope John Paul II, came to the question of sexual ethics through his experience as a university chaplain, teacher, and confessor. Those experiences taught him that the young people with whom he worked deserved a moral theory of sexuality that affirmed their vocations to sexual love, and in terms that made sense to them as modern men and women. As a faithful pastor, he was convinced that the Church's sexual ethic, properly understood, contained truths essential for human happiness and rules that guided our growth in loving sexually. He also knew that in the modern world of the sexual revolution, men and women would not accept those rules unless they understood them as guideposts pointing the way to human flourishing. The Church could no longer enforce its sexual ethic by its authority alone. The Church had to make a proposal, a set of arguments.

That is what Father Wojtyła tried to do in his first book, *Love and Responsibility*.[1] The book begins not with rules, but with a vision of human goodness and human flourishing. How, the author asks, do we become responsible lovers, so that our sexual love is an expression of genuine freedom? How does our love become what we want it to be—a fully human love?

The starting point for grappling with the ethics of sexual love, Wojtyła suggests, is the basic moral truth that we should never use another person for our own purposes, whether those purposes are wealth, ego satisfaction, power, or pleasure. The imperative not to use others is the moral basis of freedom, Wojtyła argues. Only if we live this basic moral truth can we engage and interact with others freely and generously, without reducing others to manipulable objects. When two freedoms meet each other in pursuit of something they both believe to be good—when, for example, my freedom meets your freedom as we both seek knowledge or love—then we can both say, "I'm not using you," and, "You're not using me." This is true of all human relationships, but it is especially true of love. For love is the meeting of two freedoms—my freedom and your freedom—seeking to give themselves away, to another who will receive that freedom as the gift of self. Loving, in other words, is the opposite of using.[2]

If sexual love is simply another expression of personal autonomy, of freedom understood as "doing it my way," then whatever we may know about the biological facts of life, we are missing something crucial about the moral facts of life. Everyone recognizes that it is impossible to become a good person by cutting oneself off from others. That is precisely what we do when we reduce others to objects for sexual gratification, even if that gratification is mutual and consensual. We can make love without loving, and we remain essentially, painfully alone when we do.

A sexual ethic that calls us to loving rather than using transforms sex from something that just happens into an experience that deepens our human dignity and engages our freedom. Sex that just happens, even with its transient thrills, is dehumanized sex. Sex that is the expression of the love of two persons—sex that is the meeting of two freedoms in mutual giving and receptivity—is fully human and fully humanizing.

In *Love and Responsibility,* Wojtyła proposes that the other person, not just the other body, is the recipient of a truly human act of sexual love. The goal of genuinely human sexual expression is to deepen a personal relationship. The mutual gift of sexual pleasure contributes to that deepening. In freely giving myself sexually to another person as an expression of love, I am being myself in the most radical way. I am making a gift of myself to another in a profoundly intimate expression of who I am. That kind of gift, and the receptivity able to accept it, requires permanence and commitment. One-night stands or open-ended relationships cannot achieve mutual self-giving and receptiveness. Without those deeply human characteristics, sexual love is not really love. Attraction by itself does not rise to the level of love. Attraction must be wedded to commitment if the body language of sex is to speak the truth about love. That is the profoundly humanistic reason for the moral truth that sexual love is to be expressed within the bond of marriage.

Viewed in these terms, from inside the Catholic vision of human flourishing, chastity is not a laundry list of prohibitions. Chastity is what Father Wojtyła called "the integrity of love." Chastity is the virtue that allows me to love another as a person. That is why chaste sexual love (the phrase is emphatically not a contradiction in terms) is ecstatic sexual love, in the original Greek meaning of "ecstasy": being "transported outside oneself." In chaste, committed sexual love, I put my emotional center—I put my self—in the care of another. We are made free so that we can freely dispose of ourselves as a gift to others. That is a bedrock principle of the moral life as the Catholic Church understands it. We are made free so that we can love, freely—which is to say, so that we can love truly and humanly. That is the moral truth that should frame our sexual lives.

Freedom, not prohibition, is the framework of an authentically Catholic sexual ethic. Loving versus using is the moral issue posed by the sexual revolution.

What Sex Teaches Us About God

Karol Wojtyła didn't stop thinking through the tangle of issues involved in human sexual love when he became pope. In fact, he devoted 129 general audience addresses in his first five years as Bishop of Rome to deepening his analysis of sexuality, through a compelling if demanding analysis of key biblical texts on the subject. In those addresses, John Paul II teaches that our sexuality reveals important truths not only about us but also about God. Grappling with that analysis, which the Pope calls his *Theology of the Body,* is work, but then sexuality is a complicated business. The best way to come to terms with the Catholic sexual ethic today is to work through John Paul II's *Theology of the Body.*

In his first series of audience talks, on the book of *Genesis,* John Paul takes the familiar story of Adam and Eve (*Genesis* 2–3) and asks what it teaches us about maleness and femaleness, about God's purposes for the world and for us. In this respect, the first thing the creation stories teach us is that our bodies are intrinsic to who we are. The body is not just a machine I happen to inhabit. The body through which I express myself, engage others, and live out the decisions I make is not accidental to who I am. It is through our embodiedness that we live as persons, not simply individuals.

This truth sheds light on the biblical teaching that God made man and woman in his "image and likeness" (*Genesis* 1.26). We are images of God, John Paul suggests, not just because we can think and choose but because we can give ourselves to others—because we can live in communion with others. So the "complete and definitive creation of 'man,'" the Pope writes, occurs only when God creates Eve and Adam recognizes her as a human creature like himself, although different.[3] In *Genesis,* Adam is overjoyed at this discovery. In communion with Eve, he learns that the loneliness of the human condition is overcome in that mysterious process—loving someone else—by which he is truly united to another without losing himself. In genuine loving, in a genuine gift of myself to another that is reciprocated by the other's love, my own identity is not only left intact, it is enhanced.

This rhythm of giving and receiving teaches us something crucial about ourselves. It also teaches us something crucial about God. We become "the image of God," John Paul proposes, "in the moment of communion," which satisfies the radical yearning for giving myself and receiving another that is built into us as human persons.[4] That radical giving and receiving is an image of the interior life of God, a Trinity of Persons. It is also an image of God's love in creation, for the sexual love of man and woman carries with it the gift of fertility. As God creates the world through an act of self-giving love, human beings give birth to the human future by means of self-giving sexual intimacy.

From the beginning of the human story, the creation of human beings as embodied persons—male and female, both fully human but different—is a sacramental reality. Our embodiedness as male and female makes visible the invisible. Being male and female is another rumor of angels, another signal of the transcendent. In the creation stories in *Genesis* we meet, once again, the extraordinary side of the ordinary—in this case, through our embodiedness and our sexuality.

Why, then, did Adam and Eve feel "shame" at their nakedness? They did not feel that shame, the Pope observes, when they lived in a mutuality of self-giving—when they were living freedom as giving. The "original sin" that produces shame is to treat the other as an object, as some*thing*. It is a sin not because God peremptorily declares it sinful, but because using rather than loving violates the truth about our humanity that is inscribed in us as male and female. Human flourishing, *Genesis* teaches us, depends on giving ourselves, not asserting ourselves. Mutual giving in sexual love is an icon of that great truth.

In the second part of his *Theology of the Body* John Paul takes up a text that has puzzled Christians for centuries. In the Sermon on the Mount, that charter of the Christian life in which Christ describes happiness and beatitude, Jesus says, "You have heard it said, 'You shall not commit adultery.' But I say to you that everyone who looks at a woman lustfully has already committed adultery with her in his heart" (*Matthew* 5.27–28). Isn't this an impossibly high standard (and for women as well as men, since the temptation obviously cuts both ways)? The Pope suggests that this text is, in fact, a key to a humanistic understanding of our sexuality and of the ethics of love.

The original sin, John Paul has already established, is the corruption of self-giving into self-assertion, doing it my way instead of the right way. That is what lust does. Lust is the opposite of true attraction. If I am truly attracted to someone, I want their good through the gift of myself. Lust, on the other hand, is a desire for fleeting pleasure through the use, even abuse, of the other. When a man looks lustfully rather than longingly at a woman, or a woman at a man, the other person is no longer a person; he or she is an object, something by which to satisfy a transitory need. In that kind of relationship there can be neither giving nor receptivity nor communion.

The Catholic sexual ethic, the Pope proposes, redeems sexual love from the trap of lust. Catholicism doesn't prohibit the erotic. Catholicism liberates the erotic for what John Paul calls a "full and mature spontaneity," in which the age-old attraction between the sexes is fulfilled in the mutual gift of self and the mutual affirmation of the dignity of each partner.[5] The Catholic sexual ethic doesn't try to erase desire. Rather, it seeks to channel our desires "from the heart," as John Paul puts it, so that desire reaches its true fulfillment—the communion of man and woman that is an image of God in himself and of God in relationship to the world.[6] The challenge is not simply to self-control (a psychological category) but to self-mastery (a moral category): the mastery that allows me to give myself to another intimately and in such a way that I affirm and enhance the one I love in his or her giving and receptivity.

Lived this way, in what the Beatitudes call "purity of heart," sexual love is a way to sanctify the world. Living in a communion of giving and receiving leads not just to satisfaction but to holiness, and that holiness is a reflection of the sanctity of God.[7]

John Paul takes this theme even further in the third series of audience addresses that make up his *Theology of the Body.* Marriage, he writes, is the "most ancient sacrament" because, from the beginning, marriage is the ordinary reality that reveals the extraordinary truth that God created the world in an act of love.[8] For the Christian, John Paul continues, marriage is also a sacrament, or icon, of our redemption. Since New Testament times the Church has recognized a profound image of Christ's love for his Church in the love of husband and wife. The love of Christ for the Church is not affection, nor is it pride of ownership. It is nuptial love, spousal love. Sexual love in marriage gains a new intensity of meaning in this image. For nuptial love, the Pope suggests, following St. Paul, is the human reality that best mirrors the relationship between Christ the redeemer and the people he redeemed.[9]

John Paul ends this set of reflections with his boldest statement on the true meaning of sexual love. Sexual love within the bond of marriage, the Pope writes, is an act of worship. "Conjugal life becomes . . . liturgical" when the intimate "language of the body" becomes an experience of the sacred, an experience of what God intended for the world and for us "from the beginning."[10]

At which point, we are as far from the stereotypical Catholic degradation of sexuality as it is possible to get.

IS IT JUST TOO MUCH?

Is John Paul II's *Theology of the Body*—the most powerful contemporary statement of the foundations of the Catholic sexual ethic—impossibly high-minded? Experienced married couples know that sexual love, even within the bond of faithful and fruitful marriage, is not always ecstatic. Sometimes it is rather mundane.

The Pope, who has spent tens of thousands of hours in the confessional and in counseling married couples, surely knows that. Still, he suggests, ecstasy is what sexual love should aim for and point to, even in our less-than-peak moments of loving. The thirst for the ecstatic—which is another form of the thirst for God—is built into us as sexual beings. To deny that is to deny something extremely important about ourselves, and about our loving.

Moreover, what is the alternative? Sex as contact sport isn't human, or humane, sex. Sex as contact sport is little different from animal sexuality, which is instinctive and impersonal, a matter of need. Surely the promise of sexual liberation should deliver more than that.

In his *Theology of the Body,* John Paul II has taken the primary claim of the sexual revolution seriously—and then raised the ante. A true Catholic sexual ethic, framed according to the Pope's remarkable claim that our sexual love is an icon of the life of God himself, offers the world a radical view of human sexuality. That teaching gives Catholics (and other Christians, and indeed everyone who finds profound truths in the image of the human depicted in *Genesis*) a spiritual and moral framework for understanding the vocation to sexual love and to living it fully.

Within this understanding of love and sexuality, it is possible to explore the issues in a serious way.

Engaging the Issues

Catholic teaching on issues of sexual morality is incomprehensible outside the Church's conviction that there is a vocation to sexual love that must be understood like any other Christian vocation: as a means of living the Law of the Gift, the call to self-giving inscribed in the human heart. The vocation to sexual love is one of the ways in which Christians become the kind of people who can live with God forever.

When we locate sexual ethics within the broader horizon of a genuinely humanistic ethics, an ethics of beatitude, the first moral question shifts from "What am I forbidden to do?"

to "How do I live a life of sexual love that conforms to my dignity as a human person?" From inside that context of human dignity, certain things that abuse the truth of sex are still not to be done, but they are to be avoided because they demean our dignity and wound the communion of persons that chaste sexual love is intended to enhance.

If sexual love is an expression of giving and receptivity between persons who have made a profound commitment to each other, *premarital sex* violates the dignity and integrity of love. Christians, as one moral theologian nicely puts it, make love only with people to whom they have made promises—and serious promise making, of the sort involved in the complete gift of self that sexual love represents, is not transitory or serial. *Self-abuse*, or masturbation, is sexual solipsism, and for that reason violates the integrity of the person and the integrity of love. When love is confused with self-pleasuring, our capacity to give ourselves as true lovers to another withers. *Pornography* is an abuse of sexual expression that reduces other human beings to objects for the viewer's gratification. In the illusory world of pornographic sex, a world in which women are the primary victims, no one can learn the virtues of self-giving love. *Rape* is the clearest example today of what the Church means when it teaches that there are "intrinsically evil acts," acts that are evil in themselves and that no combination of circumstances and intentions can ever justify. The forcible violation of the sexual intimacy of another person is perhaps the most profound assault on human dignity imaginable; it is, in fact, a form of torture. By its very wickedness it illustrates the truth it denies: genuinely human sexual love is always self-giving love between free human beings.

Contraception

Contraception has been a fevered issue in the Catholic Church and between the Catholic Church and the world for decades. Some clarifications on what the Church is not teaching here can help make sense of what the Church does teach about the morally appropriate way to regulate the gift of fertility.

Catholicism rejects an ideology of fertility at all costs. The Catholic Church teaches that all married couples are called to a "responsible parenthood," in which the issue is not simply avoiding another child but building a family prudently. As Pope John Paul II has written, judgments couples make about the number of children they can raise responsibly are made "before God," with a well-formed conscience. Nor, the Pope adds, is this a decision that someone else—like a government agency—can make for a couple. There can be morally compelling reasons for limiting fertility or for having larger families than a couple might at first think appropriate.[11]

The Catholic Church, in other words, teaches the moral responsibility of family planning. The issue is not whether a couple should plan their family, but how they live that plan. What is the method of regulating fertility and living responsible parenthood that best safeguards the human dignity of the spouses and honors the sacramentality of married love as mutual self-donation and receptivity? Within the Catholic concept of sexual love, using the natural rhythms of the body to regulate fertility is a more humanistic way to live procreative responsibility than using chemical or mechanical contraceptives. Following the body's rhythms honors the design built into creation by God, and it honors the truth that in marriage, man and woman are what the Pope calls the "ministers of the design" by which loving and giving life are intimately linked.[12] In a culture in which "natural" has become one of the sacred words of secular society, such a conviction deserves more than contemptuous dismissal; it deserves to be engaged.

When it is, surprising things happen. Take, for example, one testimony from a newly wed woman:

> Natural family planning [NFP] is not the justly ridiculed rhythm method, which involves vaguely guessing when the woman expects to ovulate and abstaining for a few days around day fourteen of her cycle. The full method involves charting the woman's waking temperatures, changes in cervical fluid, and the position of the cervix. These fertility signals together indicate to the woman when her body is fertile. . . .
>
> Advocates of the method point to several benefits: increased communication between partners, lack of side effects from drugs, latex, or medications, and higher efficacy rates than barrier methods (NFP is over 98 percent effective when followed correctly). We found all these to be true, and my husband . . . and I agree that NFP is one of the best decisions we have made in our marriage.
>
> But the turning point came for me as I watched, month after month, as my temperature rose and fell and my hormones marched in perfect harmony. I had no idea I was so beautiful. I found myself near tears one day looking at my chart and thinking, "Truly, I am fearfully and wonderfully made." My fertility is not a disease to be treated. It is a wonderful gift. I am a wonderful gift.[13]

In the Catholic view of things, couples grow into their love through a process that involves sexual expression and sexual abstinence, sexual ecstasy and sexual asceticism. That there will be failures in this process of growth goes—or should go—without saying. That is why the Church teaches its confessors to be mindful of the mercy of Christ, which can transform any situation, however difficult; to discuss particular problems of sexual morality within the horizon of faith and the challenge to live all of life as a gift; and to encourage those who struggle with the Church's teaching not to lose heart. As a 1997 Vatican instruction to confessors all over the world put it, even while the priest in confession challenges penitents to live the fullness of chaste sexual love, "the confessor is to avoid demonstrating lack of trust either in the grace of God or in the disposition of the penitent, by exacting humanly impossible absolute guarantees of an irreproachable future conduct."[14] If the confessor is in any doubt about these matters, he may neither delay nor deny the forgiveness of Christ and the Church.[15]

Divorce

Divorce has been a deeply, even bitterly contested issue throughout Christian history. The constant Catholic teaching on the indissolubility of marriage, so often presented and experienced in legal terms, has a profound theological root. As we have seen, in the Catholic view of things God's purposes in both creation and redemption are revealed in marriage. If a sacramental marriage, an icon of God's creative and redeeming love, is dissoluble, then, we would have to conclude, so is God's love for the world and Christ's love for the Church.[16] This does not resolve the question of what constitutes a sacramental, and thus indissoluble, marriage, but it does suggest the seriousness of what is at stake in this often painful issue.

Church law permits an "annulment"—a legal declaration that no sacramental marriage ever existed—in cases where it can be shown that either party or both did not freely consent to the marriage with sufficient knowledge of the obligations involved.[17] This practice does not satisfy those who believe that they were, in fact, truly married before but that their first marriage irretrievably broke down. Nor does it satisfactorily address the cases of men and women who want to enter a sacramental second marriage after civil divorce but who cannot provide the evidence that would result in an annulment of their first marriage according to Church law. Bishops and pastors throughout the Catholic world struggle with these questions. In a world accustomed to thinking that every problem must have a legal solution, it may seem that there must be some way to resolve this within Church law. Perhaps that is impossible. Cardinal Joseph Ratzinger has suggested that in legally intractable cases (for example, when a first spouse has maliciously refused to provide the evidence that could lead to an annulment), "experienced pastors" could perhaps make an "extrajuridical determination that the first marriage did not exist" and thus admit to communion a divorced and remarried person whose first marriage had not been canonically annulled.[18] The principle of indissolubility, the cardinal insisted, is irrevocable, but there might be pastoral resolutions of individual cases that are simply unresolvable legally.

Homosexuality

Catholic teaching on homosexual sex has been bitterly assaulted by gay rights activists, not only because most active homosexuals flatly reject what the Church teaches, but because the Catholic Church seems to be the primary institutional barrier to the legalization of gay marriage and to the legal acceptance of homosexuality as the equivalent of race under civil rights law. The Church does in fact teach that homosexual acts are morally wrong because they violate the iconography of sexual differentiation and complementarity that make sexual love possible as an act of mutual giving and reciprocity, and because they are, by their nature, incapable of being life-generating.[19] The Church does not teach that homosexuality, as an orientation, is itself sinful. It does teach what many, perhaps even most, homosexuals experience—that this form of sexual attraction is a trial and a burden.[20]

Gay activists often charge the Church with a willful failure to acknowledge their difference and with antigay "prejudice." But there is no prejudice here. The Catholic Church flatly rejects the prejudiced claim that homosexual persons are, somehow, inhuman or subhuman. In the Catholic view of things, homosexuals are human persons called to live the Law of the Gift inscribed in the human heart just like everyone else. Just like others, homosexuals in today's society will struggle to live chastely—to live the integrity of love in self-giving and to avoid sexual acts that are, by their nature, morally disordered because they are acts of self-assertion rather than self-gift. No serious Catholic imagines that this is easy for anyone. In their struggles, homosexually oriented men and women ought to find support in the Catholic Church, a Church of sinners from the beginning of its existence.

The late Cardinal John J. O'Connor of New York was a frequent target of gay animus; one catalogue of paintings about AIDS described O'Connor as a "fat cannibal" and a "creep in black skirts," and referred to St. Patrick's Cathedral as "that house of walking swastikas on Fifth Avenue." The cardinal, for his part, refused to deny what the Church taught about the morality of homosexual acts. At the same time, he embraced the demands of charity and solidarity enjoined by that same Catholic teaching. And so the cardinal archbishop of New York regularly visited one of the hospices sponsored by the archdiocese to comfort, counsel with, and change the bedpans of dying AIDS patients.

That is what the Catholic Church is about, in this and other matters of sexual morality. The Church teaches the truth it believes it has been given and stands in solidarity with human beings who fall and struggle to rise again—just like Christ on the way of the cross. The two go together.

7

Why Do We Suffer?

Redeeming the World and Its Pain

It's one of the hardest facts of life to face or understand. As you're reading this chapter, children are suffering from hideous diseases or being abused by their parents; prisoners are being tortured by despotic regimes; women will be raped; spouses will assault each other; reputations will be ruined for political purposes; good people will die too young and bad people will live on. "Why?" is the obvious question.

The ubiquity of suffering has long been considered an argument against the existence of a good God. To say that God "permits" suffering seems to make God either an incompetent or a sadist. Many find it easier to reconcile the unavoidable realities of suffering with an accidental and purposeless universe than to accept the traditional biblical answer to the problem: suffering, like evil, is the reverse side of freedom, at least as human beings have lived their God-given freedom since Adam and Eve. A world of freedom is a world in which things can, and do, go wrong.

Over the centuries, human beings have coped with suffering in various ways: stoic resignation, angry protest, numb silence, fervent prayer, quests for the miraculous. Reconciling ourselves to the inevitability of suffering—finding meaning in suffering—is particularly difficult today. In a culture dominated by the pleasure principle, it is very hard to make sense of suffering, which seems both needless and antithetical to human flourishing and happiness. Modern medicine's success in relieving pain has made us less familiar with suffering in its most basic physical form; a friend once remarked that in looking at any painting of a major historical scene prior to the twentieth century, one ought to remember that at least half the people in the painting were suffering atrocious toothache. Although there is certainly good in medicine's capacity to manage physical suffering—no one with access to properly trained medical personnel need die in excruciating pain—advances in biotechnology hold out the promise of taking things to an entirely different level. At the beginning of the third millennium, geneticists and biotechnology executives talk about engineering virtually immortal human beings, freed from any serious pain or suffering.

Are Catholics fated to spend the rest of human history trying to explain, to an increasingly uncomprehending world, that suffering is good for us?

Two generations ago, Catholicism had an answer to a very basic human question: what do you tell a youngster facing the terrors of the dentist's chair? The answer was "Offer it up to God, for the souls in purgatory or in reparation for your own sins." That stock answer (which is almost never heard these days) strikes many Catholics today as lying somewhere between quaint and cruel. Perhaps there was something more going on here, though. For that answer attempted to link our suffering here and now to the redemptive suffering of Christ, and to the purification that the grace of Christ can work in our own lives and the lives of our dead friends and relatives. That is no small thing. Besides, as a famous Catholic writer of liberal disposition once said in criticizing the contemporary Catholic loss of a sense of redemptive suffering, "What else are you going to tell the kid as the dentist comes at him with that drill?"

Suffering, in the Catholic view of things, is a mystery. By "mystery," Catholic theology means not a puzzle to be solved as Sherlock Holmes would do, but a reality that can only be grasped and comprehended in an act of love. There is no "answer" to the problem of suffering in the sense that there are answers to questions like "Was Alger Hiss guilty?" or "What is two plus two?" The Church has always believed and taught that there is a different kind of answer to the question "Why do we suffer?" That answer takes us directly into the heart of the Church, which is Jesus Christ.

That Jesus Christ is a suffering redeemer has been a shock and an offense since the first days of Christianity. The challenge of belief in a redeemer whose victorious strength is displayed in his weakness may be greater today than at any other time in the past two thousand years, given our culture's resistance to the idea that suffering is the necessary path to beatitude or human flourishing.

But that is the mystery—the profoundly human mystery—of suffering. Dogs and cats and pandas feel pain. Only human beings suffer. That fact should suggest that there is a link between suffering and the essence of our humanity. Pondering that link is an opening into the entire Catholic story about the world and about us. In that story we meet an even more astonishing proposal. God's answer to suffering is not to avoid it, or deny it, or blame it on human folly. God's answer to suffering is to embrace it—to enter the world in the person of his Son, to redeem suffering *through* suffering.

No Accidents

Pope John Paul II has an intimate familiarity with suffering. His mother died when he was nine, and his older brother when Karol Wojtyła was twelve. As a young man he saw his professors shipped off to concentration camps. For several years he walked five kilometers to work through freezing winter weather, to break rocks in a quarry or carry buckets of lime in a dingy factory while the Nazis murdered many of his friends. His father died, leaving him an orphan in an occupied country. He was run over by a German army truck and left unconscious in a ditch. He lost his closest friend when he was fifty. Another old friend suffered a massive stroke hours before Karol Wojtyła entered the conclave that elected him pope. He was shot at point-blank range by an assassin in his front yard in 1981, and after surviving emergency surgery, he was almost killed by a tainted blood transfusion that reduced him to a shell of his former self for months. He broke his hip and the prosthesis didn't work properly. He developed a neurological disorder, akin to Parkinson's disease, that made it difficult for this lifelong athlete to walk. Beyond these physical burdens, there is the spiritual suffering he accepts as one facet of his office. The Pope receives prayer requests from all over the world. The household nuns type them onto sheets of paper that are placed in the prie-dieu where John Paul takes ninety minutes for private prayer at the beginning of every day. There, on those sheets, he confronts the world's suffering in microcosm, even as he confronts it during his workday in the arena of world politics. This is a man who knows suffering from the inside.

When John Paul II writes about the meaning of suffering in Christian perspective, he is worth listening to. There is no avoidance here. For John Paul II to avoid the realities of suffering would be to deny his own experience.

Six weeks after meeting with his would-be assassin in a Roman prison cell, John Paul published an apostolic letter entitled *Salvifici Doloris* [Salvific Suffering]. The letter begins with the observation that suffering is a universal human experience. Suffering is an entire human world, and no one can avoid passing through it. Everyone suffers. There is no escape from the questions "Why?" and "What for?"

Suffering, the Pope suggests, cannot be merely accidental. The universality of the experience of suffering suggests that suffering "seems to be particularly essential to the nature of man."[1] Our suffering is not mere animal pain. In addition to physical suffering, human beings experience "moral suffering," the "pain of the soul."[2] When we betray or are betrayed, when we are denied what is justly due us, when we lash out and wound someone we love, when we are wounded ourselves by a friend or relative, our pain is not just psychological. It is spiritual. Men and women can be wounded deeply, in the depths of their persons, by the death of a child, a parent, a spouse, a friend of the heart.

This experience of moral suffering tells us something important about ourselves. It tells us that we have a soul, not just a psyche. Suffering, John Paul is suggesting, is a signal of transcendence. In what seems to be the devil's work, we can detect another rumor of angels. Suffering, the Pope writes, is "one of those points in which man is in a certain sense 'destined' to go beyond himself."[3] Suffering is not just an unsettling human problem. It is a profound human mystery. Just as with the mystery of love or the mystery of insight, we meet God through the mystery of suffering.

Redemptive Suffering

The Bible, John Paul notes, is a "great book about suffering." In it we encounter many instances of that "pain of the soul" which is the worst form of human suffering: the death of one's children, the fear of annihilation, barrenness, exile, persecution and mockery, loneliness and betrayal, the prosperity of the wicked amid the misery of the just, unfaithfulness and ingratitude. Suffering, in the biblical world, clearly has to do with evil. We suffer when we experience evil.

Still, the Christian conviction, drawn from the first chapter of the Hebrew Bible, is that creation is essentially good.

Evil is not a coprinciple of creation, as in other ancient religious systems. If the world God created is essentially good and yet there is evil in the world, evil and good must be somehow related. Evil, John Paul writes, "is a certain lack, limitation, or distortion of good."[4] Illness is a deprivation of health; a lie is a distortion of the truth. We suffer, the Pope suggests, because of evil, but that very suffering points us toward a good. Suffering is caught up in the interplay of good and evil in the world. Suffering is enmeshed in the mystery of human freedom.

The Bible sometimes describes suffering as a punishment for the evil we do, but that punishment, the Pope suggests, is also linked to good. The punishment "creates the possibility of rebuilding goodness" in the person who suffers. This, John Paul underlines, "is an extremely important aspect of suffering." Suffering opens up possibilities for the breakthrough of good, for "conversion," for our becoming the kind of people who can enjoy beatitude with God, because we "recognize the divine mercy in this call to repentance."[5]

Still, the Pope suggests, the mystery of suffering is not ultimately susceptible to rational explanation. However elegantly constructed, our explanations leave us dissatisfied. Something seems missing. That missing something, the Pope suggests, is in fact some*one:* Jesus Christ.

God's love, which was so great that it burst the boundaries of God's inner life and poured itself forth in creation, is "the ultimate source of the meaning of everything that exists," including, of course, the meaning of suffering. Learning that "love is . . . the fullest source of the answer to the question of the meaning of suffering" requires not a rational argument, but a demonstration. That is what God has "given . . . in the cross of Jesus Christ."[6]

The entire life of Christ points inexorably toward the cross. Jesus' human life is a growth into the world of suffering to which he responds by his healings. Those healings, both physical and psychological, are signs that the Kingdom of God, a world beyond suffering, is breaking into this world. Yet even as he heals the suffering, Christ suffers. He experiences exhaustion, homelessness, the misunderstanding of those closest to him. When Peter rebukes Jesus for saying that he must go to Jerusalem and suffer, Jesus turns on the fisherman and calls him "Satan" (*Matthew* 16.23). Slowly, relentlessly, the net of hostility closes around Jesus, and the crux of the matter is at hand: the moment in which to link suffering to love in the passion of the cross.[7]

Christ's was an "incomparable depth and intensity of suffering." Christ suffers as a man, but "insofar as the man who suffers is in person the only begotten Son himself," John Paul writes, Christ's suffering has a cosmic and divine density that is "capable of embracing the measure of evil" contained in the whole of human history.[8] As the Swiss theologian Hans Urs von Balthasar puts it in almost frightening language, we cannot imagine what agonies that entailed. What it would mean to "bear the burden of the world's guilt, to experience in oneself the inner perversion of a humankind that refuses any sort of service, any sort of respect, to God" is beyond our comprehension.[9] We cannot imagine the suffering involved when the Son takes on himself all that the Father finds abominable. Yet that is what Christ suffers on the cross.

In Christ on the cross, we meet the triune God's

"eternal . . . plan . . . to clear out all the refuse of the world's sin by burning it in the fire of suffering love." Christ's passion is the embodiment in history of "the fire that has burned eternally in God as [a] blazing passion," the passion of resolute and radical love. God burns for the world to enter into this divine passion. For that to happen, the burning love of God in himself must reach out to the world and redeem it by consuming everything in the world that is incapable of love, including evil and suffering.

That is what happens on the cross when, in obedience to the Father and in the most profound act of self-giving love, the Son takes all the world's evil upon himself, including the evil of death. On the cross, Balthasar writes, two eternal realities meet: "God's fury, which will make no compromises with sin but can only reject it and burn it to ashes, and God's love, which begins to reveal itself precisely at the place of this inexorable confrontation."[10] The cross is not the end of the story. On the cross, evil and death are overcome through redemptive suffering. Christ conquers suffering by his "obedience unto death," which the Father vindicates in the resurrection.[11]

In the mystery of God's love, burning its way through the world and through history, the moment of catastrophe is, in truth, the moment of liberation.

Weakness and Strength

With the passion of Christ, John Paul II suggests, "all human suffering has found itself in a new situation."

Not only is humanity redeemed by suffering; human suffering itself is redeemed.[12] Since Christ suffered in place of us and for us, every human being has a share in the redemption he accomplished. Everyone is "called to share in that suffering . . . through which all human suffering has been redeemed." On the cross, through his suffering, Christ "raised human suffering to the level of redemption." Because of that, every human being, in his or her suffering, can "become a sharer in the redemptive suffering of Christ."[13]

When Christ became a participant in human suffering, he enabled us to have a share in his redemption. When we discover, by faith, the redemptive quality of Christ's suffering, we discover the redemptive nature of our own suffering.[14] By linking our suffering with his, our suffering, like his, becomes linked to love. And that is the answer to the youngster in the dentist's chair.

In identifying our suffering with Christ's, St. Paul teaches, we are being prepared for "an eternal weight of glory, beyond all comparison" (*2 Corinthians* 4.17). Suffering, transformed by the cross of Christ, passes over from an irrationality or an absurdity to become another means by which we grow into the kind of people who can live with God forever. Christ conquers suffering and death not by asserting himself, but by making himself utterly vulnerable; in his weakness was his power, and in his humiliation lay his greatness.[15] In Christ's suffering, Pope John Paul writes, we learn again about the Law of the Gift written into the human heart as an expression of our being made in the image of God: "In [Christ], God has confirmed his desire to act especially through suffering, which is man's weakness and emptying of self, and he wishes to make his power known precisely in this weakness and emptying of self."[16] That is why, with St. Paul, we can rejoice in our sufferings, even those that seem to wound us most deeply. For the more we share in the love of Christ manifest in Christ's suffering, the more we rediscover the soul we thought we had lost because of our suffering.[17]

This paradox of weakness and strength, displayed on the cross of Christ, helps explain two of the most puzzling passages in the New Testament: St. Paul's assertion "When I am weak, then I am strong" (*2 Corinthians* 12.10) and Paul's claim that, in his sufferings, "I complete what is lacking in Christ's afflictions for the sake of his body, that is, the Church" (*Colossians* 1.24). If the truth of Christ's self-emptying is vindicated in the resurrection, John Paul suggests, then "the weaknesses of all human suffering are capable of being infused with the same power of God manifested in Christ's cross." In opening ourselves to the power of the cross by identifying our suffering with Christ's, our suffering becomes a vehicle by which to continue in the world "the salvific powers of God offered to humanity in Christ." Christ redeemed the world "completely and to the very limit," but the world has not yet experienced the fullness of its redemption. Through our suffering, Christ constantly opens himself to every human suffering; through our suffering, "what is lacking" in the world's experience of its redemption is being completed. That is how "human suffering, by reason of the loving union with Christ, completes the suffering of Christ." Our suffering completes Christ's suffering "just as the Church completes the redemptive work of Christ," by extending it in time and history.[18]

The Vocation of Suffering

If Mary, the mother of Jesus, is the model of all discipleship in the Church, then Mary at the foot of the cross is the paradigm of the relationship between suffering and discipleship. If Mary's first "yes" to God's invitation was made in joy—"My soul magnifies the Lord, and my spirit rejoices in God my Savior" (*Luke* 1.46–47)—then Mary's second "yes" is given in silence, when she stands in mute sorrow on Calvary, experiencing the suffering foretold by the old priest Simeon shortly after the birth of Christ: "And a sword will pierce through your own soul, too" (*Luke* 2.35). The mother of Jesus embodies the full weight of Christ's own challenge to discipleship: "If anyone would come after me, let him deny himself and take up his cross daily and follow me" (*Luke* 9.23).

And here, the question "Why do we suffer?" is reframed. With Mary, we silently ask "Why?" to the one on the cross, the one who is already suffering. And as Pope John Paul writes, "Christ does not answer directly and he does not answer in the abstract." We hear Christ's answer "as he allows us to become sharers in his suffering."[19] Suffering, for the Christian, is not an anomaly. Suffering is a vocation.

Because it is a vocation, suffering can be a means of service, of making ourselves into a gift, indirectly or directly. Indirectly, as the Pope writes, suffering, united to the cross of Christ, "clears the way for the grace which transforms human souls" and supports the "spiritual powers of good" in the ongoing struggle against evil.[20] Directly, the vocation of suffering is modeled on the parable of the good Samaritan (*Luke* 10. 29–37).

To live the example of the good Samaritan means to be available to others in their suffering. The Samaritan's stopping by the roadside at the sight of the man beaten by robbers "does not mean curiosity, but availability." The name "good Samaritan," John Paul notes, is widely used for anyone who is sensitive to others' suffering. If Christ emphasizes this compassion—"Go and do likewise," Jesus says at the end of the parable—then compassion, the ability to suffer with someone else, is an essential component of the vocation of suffering.

Through this gospel story, John Paul suggests, we gain another insight into the mystery of suffering. As we have seen, suffering helps shape each of us individually for beatitude as suffering helps us enter personally into the mystery of Christ's redemptive cross. Suffering is also present in the world "in order to unleash love in the human person, that unselfish gift of one's 'I' on behalf of other people." The world of suffering, John Paul proposes, "calls for . . . another world: the world of human love." In a paradoxical way, we owe something to others' suffering. Suffering draws us outside ourselves and draws out of us self-giving and unselfish love. Like the good Samaritan, we live the vocation of suffering by means of what the Pope calls a "fundamental human solidarity," through love of neighbor. We cannot "indifferently pass by the suffering of another."[21] We must stop and show compassion; we must stop and "suffer with"; we must stop and make ourselves into a gift for another. Through Christ's redemption, "suffering is present in the world in order to release love, in order to give birth to works of love toward neighbor, in order to transform the whole of human civilization into a 'civilization of love.'"[22]

"Those who share in the sufferings of Christ," the Pope concludes, "preserve in their own sufferings a very special particle of the infinite treasure of the world's redemption." Because of that, we can "share this treasure with others."[23] Because of that, the Christian must share the treasure.

The Final Act

In the Catholic view of things, suffering is integral to the drama of the human story. To ponder the mystery of suffering through the prism of faith is to learn something about God and about God's redemption of the world. John Paul II insists that everyone who enters the mystery of suffering "discovers himself, his own humanity, his own dignity, his own mission."[24] Christ, the redeemer who saves through suffering, "fully reveals man to himself and makes his supreme calling clear," as the bishops of Vatican II taught.[25]

The mystery of suffering leads, finally, to the mystery of the Kingdom: to the complete vindication of God's gift of himself in history, which enters history in a definitive way in Jesus Christ. As philosopher Peter Kreeft writes, things look different "when history is seen as his-story." Suffering becomes the bass note "in a harmony whose high notes are lost in heaven."[26] And the promise of what that heaven will entail is given by the man to whom the dying Christ confided the care of his mother, the first disciple—the apostle John, in his vision of the Kingdom come in its glory:

> Then I saw a new heaven and a new earth; for the first heaven and the first earth had passed away, and the sea was no more. And I saw the holy city, new Jerusalem, coming down out of heaven from God, prepared as a bride adorned for her husband; and I heard a loud voice from the throne say, "Behold, the dwelling of God is with men. He will dwell with them, and they shall be his people, and God himself will be with them; he will wipe away every tear from their eyes, and death will be no more, neither shall there be mourning nor crying nor pain anymore, for the former things have passed away." And he who sat upon the throne said, "Behold, I make all things new." (*Revelation* 21.1–5)

That is the Catholic vision of things. We learn it through suffering.

8

What About the Rest of the World?

Other Christians, Other Religions

The Catholic Church, like just about every other institution, was a target of the wicked humor of comedian Lenny Bruce, a hero of the sixties counterculture. "There's only one Church that's 'The Church,'" Bruce used to crack, "and that's the Catholic Church." Buried inside what was meant to be a put-down is a rich theological insight.

The Catholic Church's belief that Jesus Christ is the unique savior of the world and that Christ's mission continues in a unique way in the Catholic Church makes Catholicism a discomforting presence in some parts of our twenty-first-century world. That all truths are equal, so long as they're sincerely held, is about all that today's high culture can offer in answer to Pontius Pilate's question "Truth? What is truth?" (*John* 18.38). If sincerity, not reality, is the measure of truth, however, truth is ephemeral, a mere cognitive or psychological construct. To say, "All truths are equal," is to say that there is no truth in the sense of *the* truth.

To which some would surely add, "And a good thing, too." Isn't a deep, unshakable conviction that one possesses the truth an invitation to arrogance and aggression? Didn't the Crusades and the Inquisition and witch burning and the Thirty Years' War and the rest of the parade of horribles start just that way? Isn't a principled, humane skepticism the better way to a more peaceful world?

When not being cited to suggest that Catholicism is unsafe for world peace or for civility within pluralistic democracies, Catholic convictions about the truth of Christ and the Church are also used to raise questions about the Catholic commitment to ecumenism (the search for unity among Christian communions) and interreligious dialogue (the search for truth between Christians and Jews, and among Christians, Jews, Muslims, Buddhists, Hindus, and others). If the Catholic Church believes itself to be the most complete expression in history of the one, true Church of Jesus Christ, how can it be in open dialogue with other Christian communities? If Christ is the unique savior of the world and his Church continues that saving mission today, why would the Catholic Church be interested in dialogue with other world religions, except as a subtle ruse for seeking converts? Isn't the Catholic claim to a singular grasp of the truth of things the kind of fanaticism that makes conversation difficult, if not impossible? Isn't a healthy reticence about one's own convictions the starting point for serious engagement with the convictions of others?

The questions sound so sensible. From inside the Catholic Church's understanding of itself and its mission, however, they seem a good illustration of poet e. e. cummings's insight: "Always the more beautiful answer to him who asks the more beautiful question." There can't be a good answer to the question of Christian unity if Christians ignore the promise of Christ: that his disciples "will know the truth, and the truth will make you free" (*John* 8.32). Nor are we likely to find a good solution to the many social and political problems posed by the facts of difference and plurality in a world without truth. For a world without truth is simply a world of power, in which the "truth" of the stronger gets imposed on the weaker.

It helps to think about this in terms of the kind of people with whom you'd like to have a conversation about important things. Who is more likely to respect the convictions of others—someone whose relativism compels him to view all convictions skeptically, or someone whose conviction teaches him that respect for others is a religious and moral imperative, even when we disagree about the most serious things? What is a better definition of tolerance—avoiding differences as if they were of no consequence, or engaging differences in a respectful conversation we believe to be a moral duty?

Beyond these issues, there is the rubble of history, and it, too, can raise questions about the Catholic commitment to the kind of dialogue that makes ecumenism and interreligious encounter possible. It is not within the scope of this small book to explore some of the new historical evidence that is changing our view of alleged Catholic fanaticism and its deleterious role in history. Some of this evidence has emerged from studies sponsored by the Catholic Church itself, at the insistence of Pope John Paul II, as a preparation for the jubilee year of 2000. From these and other historical explorations, we have been reminded that the Crusades were, among many other things, an effort to protect Christian pilgrims in what were, for centuries, historically Christian lands. We have learned that some of those under suspicion in sixteenth-century Spain preferred to be tried in the religious courts of the Inquisition rather than in the civil courts because they believed the Inquisition's courts were much more just. We have been reminded that in the Galileo affair, the Church stood with the scientific consensus of the time. We have been reminded that aspects of the Reformation in England, Germany, and elsewhere were motivated by commercial and political concerns, not by pious convictions about the essential reform of Christ's Church. History, it seems, is a lot more complicated, and a lot more interesting, when one breaks through the stereotypes and discovers things as they were.

The point here, though, is to explore the Catholic Church's ecumenical commitment to the quest for Christian unity and the Church's commitment to dialogue with the great world religions. These are, in fact, two distinct questions, and it often confuses things to conflate them. In this instance they belong together because both touch on the important question of truth and its relationship to pluralism, civility, and respect for the convictions of others.

A final preliminary point: the Catholic Church believes that ecumenism and interreligious dialogue are not like old-fashioned labor negotiations. Ecumenism and interreligious dialogue are not, in other words, zero-sum games, in which one side's loss is necessary for the other's gain. Unfortunately, this is the way such dialogues are often understood, even within the dialogues. If the Catholic Church would only give, say, on the question of women and the ordained ministry, then Protestants, satisfied that they'd won that point, might be prepared to give on, say, a larger role for the papacy in a reunified Christianity. If the Catholic Church would just give a bit on the unique salvific role of Jesus Christ, then Muslims or Buddhists or Hindus could concede that Jesus might be the savior of Christians, if not their own savior. It sounds reasonable—if you think religious truth claims are of little consequence, or if you think that there is no such thing as truth. From the Catholic point of view, as from the point of view of religiously committed and theologically informed Protestant and Orthodox Christians, and of serious Jews, Muslims, Hindus, and Buddhists, the labor negotiation model of ecumenism and interreligious dialogue doesn't work. The issues don't cut that way. If there are truths at stake, then anyone's loss is everyone's loss, and a gain of insight is everyone's gain.

Ecumenism and interreligious dialogue aren't zero-sum exercises in which the very play of the game defines winners and losers. But what are these dialogues, from the Catholic point of view?

Christ Creates Unity

The modern ecumenical movement began in 1910 at a great missionary conference of world Protestant leaders held in Edinburgh. At first the movement's goal was to promote cooperation rather than competition in the colonial world of Protestant missions. Within a decade or so, the movement began to seek a common Christian position on the social, political, and economic issues of the day. This led, in turn, to Faith and Order conferences that explicitly tackled questions of doctrine and "polity"—the organization, or "order," of the Church and its ministry. After the Second World War, the ecumenical movement found a bureaucratic center for all these enterprises in the World Council of Churches, headquartered in Geneva.

The Catholic Church became formally involved with the ecumenical movement through the Second Vatican Council. Pope John XXIII, passionately concerned with Christian unity, invited Protestant and Orthodox observers to the Council and established a Secretariat for Christian Unity within the Roman Curia. In the immediate aftermath of the Council, a kind of ecumenical euphoria reigned. The eleventh-century breach between Rome and the Orthodox Churches of the Christian East and the sixteenth-century ecumenical fracture of Western Christianity appeared to be on the verge of healing and closure. Within a few years, that euphoria had burned out, and it seemed that the organic reconstitution of a unified Christianity lay just as far in the future as ever. In the decades after Vatican II, a series of bilateral ecumenical dialogues—Anglican/Roman Catholic, Lutheran/Roman Catholic, Orthodox/Roman Catholic, Reformed/Roman Catholic—made considerable progress on clarifying painful historical questions and certain doctrinal issues. These dialogues reached a climax in 1999, when the Catholic Church and the Lutheran World Federation jointly affirmed that, despite continuing differences in theological understanding, they held in common the truths involved in the doctrine that we are justified by grace through faith in Christ—the issue that launched the Lutheran Reformation in 1517.

Yet the hard fact remained that Lutherans and Catholics were no closer to ecclesial reunion in 1999 than they were in 1969. What had once seemed the core issue separating these communities—the doctrine of justification by faith—turned out not to have been the key to resolving other difficulties and reconstituting the unity of the Church. Similarly, by the late 1980s it became painfully clear that the Anglican/Roman Catholic dialogue had not moved the two communities closer to ecclesial reunion. This in turn raised serious questions about the claim, common throughout the twentieth century, that the English Reformation had been an essentially political separation and that there were no grave doctrinal issues between Anglicans and Roman Catholics.

Meanwhile, as these new difficulties were coming into clearer focus, the old ecumenical movement centered on the World Council of Churches abandoned the movement's original goal: the reconstitution of Christian unity through common doctrine and a mutual recognition of ministries. In 1995, the WCC's general secretary formally proposed a "paradigm shift" in which the ecumenical movement would "close the books over our past struggles" and be reconstituted as a global campaign against poverty, war, and environmental degradation.

Sociologist Peter Rossi used to say that "there are many ironies in the fire," a point graphically illustrated by the "new paradigm" proposal from Geneva. For this dramatic shift left the Catholic Church—long thought to be the tardy and fractious child in the ecumenical family—as the only global institution still committed to the ecumenical movement's classic goal: the recomposition of the unity of Christ's Church in doctrine and practice.

Amid these disappointments, setbacks, and confusions, what does the Catholic Church actually believe and teach about Christian unity? In the documents of the Second Vatican Council and in the teaching of John Paul II, the Catholic Church has proposed a vision of the ecumenical task that is both faithful to the original goal of the world ecumenical movement and to Christ's teaching that truth is at the center of Christianity. That vision is theologically, not politically, driven, which is how it must be if the Church is what it is—the Church, and not just another voluntary organization with a cause. The Catholic ecumenical vision and the Catholic understanding of other Christian communities can perhaps best be laid out as a series of propositions:

- There is only one Church because there is only one Christ, and the Church is his Body.[1]
- Christians don't create Christian unity. Christ creates the unity of the Church.[2]
- The unity of that one Church is a gift of Christ that has never been revoked, for Christ does not break his promises.[3]
- The ecumenical task is to bring that unity, which already exists in Christ, into more complete historical expression through a mutual recognition of the truths by which Christ constituted his Church.[4] In trying to give fuller expression in history to the unity Christians already enjoy, the only unity worth developing is unity in the truth; for truth, like unity, is Christ's gift to his one Church.

◆ The triumph of twentieth-century Catholic, Orthodox, and Protestant martyrs, who commonly witnessed to the truth of God in Christ and now live together in complete fellowship, united in the communion of saints in heaven that is the Church in glory, demonstrates that there is an already existing unity in the one Church of Christ.[5]

◆ The one Church of Christ "subsists" in the Catholic Church; that is, the Catholic Church understands itself to be the fullest, most rightly ordered expression in history of the Church of Christ, which transcends history.[6]

◆ The one Church of Christ is not completely identical with the Catholic Church: it does not "stop" at the boundaries of the Catholic Church. The Catholic Church believes and teaches that there are "many elements of sanctification and of truth" in Christian communities that lie outside Catholicism's visible borders.[7]

◆ Neither the presence of the one Church of Christ in its fullest historical form in the Catholic Church nor the elements of truth and sanctification present in other Christian communities should lead to a sense of Catholic satisfaction or complacency. Rather, they are imperatives pressing the Catholic Church to pursue more complete and visible Christian unity. Through prayer, theological dialogue, and common service to the world, the now-divided elements of the one Church of Christ are undergoing a reciprocal process of purification.[8]

◆ Catholics have hundreds of millions of brothers and sisters in Christ who live their Christian lives outside the formal structure of the Catholic Church. Those brothers and sisters in Christ are, in some sense, in communion with the Catholic Church. For all the baptized, from the Catholic point of view, are part of the Catholic Church, as Catholics are part of them.[9] (Again, the analogy is to the members of a body, not the members of a club.)

◆ Whether other Christians think of Catholics as brothers and sisters in Christ, Catholics have no choice but to think of other Christians that way. The Catholic Church has a unique position in world Christianity: it is the only Christian communion whose self-understanding demands that it be in ecumenical conversation with everybody else, without exception.

◆ As the ecumenical dialogue in which the Catholic Church must participate unfolds, it will become clear that recomposing, or giving fuller historical expression to, the unity that Christ gave his Church will be less difficult with some Christian communities than with others. Closest to the Catholic Church, and thus closer to the possibility of embodying that unity in the one bread and the one cup, are those Christian communities which have maintained an episcopal structure, apostolic succession in the ordination of bishops, and a sacramental (or iconic) concept of priesthood.[10]

◆ Prayer among separated brothers and sisters in Christ is "the soul of the whole ecumenical movement" and a "common invitation to Christ himself to visit the community of those who call upon him."[11]

◆ The Office of Peter is part of Christ's will for his Church. How that office is exercised is an urgent subject for ecumenical discussion. As Pope John Paul II has written, the Bishop of Rome and successor of Peter must "find a way of exercising the primacy which, while in no way renouncing what is essential to its mission, is nonetheless open to a new situation." The Catholic Church recognizes, and asks forgiveness for, all the times when the papacy has been a source of Christian disunity. The Catholic Church invites, indeed urges, other Christians to help think through a papacy that could serve their needs, based on the communion that already exists among Christians.[12] The Catholic Church also invites other Christians to think with Catholics about how Christ's promise to preserve his Church in the truth is given concrete effect in the Church. For that is the promise that grounds the Catholic belief that the Bishop of Rome can, in certain well-defined circumstances, teach infallibly on matters of faith and morals.

That is how the Catholic Church thinks about other Christians and about the quest for Christian unity.

Christians and Jews: A Divinely Mandated Entanglement

Then there is the question of the Catholic Church and the Jewish people.

At the beginning of the third millennium of Christian history, Catholics and Jews are poised on the verge of a new dialogue, of a sort not seen since the Jesus movement broke with what later became rabbinic Judaism around the time of the First Jewish War (c. A.D. 70). One key to making that dialogue succeed—and to giving a new historical meaning to the divinely mandated entanglement of Christians and Jews of which St. Paul wrote in *Romans* 9–11—is to recognize what has changed in the often tortuous history of the Catholic Church and Judaism, and why.

Some veterans of the dialogue since Vatican II, both Jews and Catholics, imagine that the agenda for Jewish-Catholic conversation has just about been completed. Things have certainly changed dramatically in the decades since Pope John XXIII and the Second Vatican Council revolutionized the relationship between Catholics and Jews by removing offensive references to Judaism from the Church's liturgy, by rejecting the deicide charge against the Jewish people, and by condemning anti-Semitism. Catholic religious-education texts now emphasize Jesus' Jewish consciousness and the Church's debt to its Jewish heritage. Tolerance and civility are understood to be the moral baseline for intergroup relations in society. The Church has begun to cleanse its conscience about the complex relationship between Christian teaching and the Holocaust. The Holy See has full diplomatic relations with the state of Israel. In the view of some veterans of the dialogue, that just about finishes the agenda.

Suppose that the opposite is the case. Suppose that the most important items on the Catholic-Jewish agenda are just coming into focus.

The welcome advances in Jewish-Catholic relations since Vatican II, coupled with the extraordinary reservoir of goodwill built up among the Jewish people by Pope John Paul II, have put Catholics and Jews on the threshold of an entirely new relationship. Catholics and Jews are now poised to pick up the conversation that ended more than nineteen hundred years ago—to open an intense theological dialogue for the first time since the parting of the ways in the first century of the common era.

This is what John Paul II has been anticipating throughout a pontificate notable for its unprecedented accomplishments in Jewish-Catholic relations. The Pope's regular meetings with local Jewish communities around the world; his steady condemnation of the sin of anti-Semitism; his historic visit to the synagogue of Rome in April 1986; his completion of full diplomatic relations between the Holy See and the state of Israel; his prayer at the Western Wall of the Temple in Jerusalem—all these things, good in their own right, have been part of a systematic attempt to clear the ground of the debris of centuries so that the most urgent conversation—the theological conversation—between Catholics and Jews can start again.

The Pope believes this is a religious obligation for Catholics. On many occasions he has said that the Church cannot think about herself without thinking about Judaism. From the Catholic point of view, Judaism is not another "world religion," but a religion intrinsic to our own, without which Christianity is inconceivable.[13] Jews, John Paul insists, are our elder brothers and sisters in the faith. John Paul, like St. Paul in *Romans,* teaches that God's covenant with "Abraham's stock" is irrevocable; John Paul also believes that Jews and Christians have a singular mandate to bring one fruit of that covenant, the Ten Commandments, to a morally stricken and confused world. For all of these reasons, a theological dialogue between Catholics and Jews is imperative.

It will take some hard work to get this new conversation started. Jews will wonder whether "theological dialogue" is code language for proselytization. At the beginning of a new century, the American Jewish community, which is the only community in the Jewish world large enough and secure enough to engage this kind of dialogue, is preoccupied with crucial debates about its own character and its demographically precarious future. In these circumstances it may seem untimely, even odd, for Catholics to suggest to their Jewish friends that it's time to get serious about a theological dialogue with the Catholic Church. Moreover, Christianity does not have a place in Jewish understanding parallel to the place that Judaism has in Christian identity.

Yet some of the finest Jewish minds of the twentieth century—Martin Buber, Franz Rosenzweig, Abraham Joshua Heschel—once turned their minds to the question of where Christianity (whose Bible, liturgy, and basic theological approach to reality are all legacies from the Jewish people) fits into a Jewish view of God's plan for the world's salvation. Some of today's leading Jewish thinkers have taken up the issue. In September 2000, 170 North American Jewish scholars and religious leaders issued a statement on Christians and Christianity entitled "Speak the Truth" (in Hebrew, "Dabru Emet"), containing eight points:

- Jews and Christians worship the same God.
- Jews and Christians seek authority and draw similar lessons from the same book, the Hebrew Bible.
- Christians can respect the Jewish claim upon the land of Israel.
- Jews and Christians share the same basic moral law,

including a commitment to the sanctity and dignity of every human life.

- Nazism was not a Christian phenomenon, although Christian anti-Jewish prejudice prepared the ground for Nazi anti-Semitism.
- The differences between Jews and Christians will not be resolved until God redeems the entire world.
- A new religious dialogue with Christians will not weaken Jewish practice or accelerate Jewish assimilation.
- Jews and Christians must work together for justice and peace.

These points hold out the promise of a newly enriched religious encounter between Catholicism and its parent, living Judaism.[14]

Election, covenant, messianic hope—to think that Jews and Catholics are now poised to pick up the conversation on these questions that was tragically interrupted more than nineteen hundred years ago is at the same time thrilling and humbling. Its possibility also challenges some conventional wisdom: that the only Christians safe for Jews are Christians who have essentially abandoned Christ; that the only state safe for Jews outside Israel is a thoroughly secular state; that Judaism can have a future as an ethnic group with liberal political commitments, making common cause with Christians of similar political convictions. There is no security for Jews, however, and there is no enlightenment for Catholics in a dialogue between a religiously hollow Judaism and a religiously hollow Christianity. The Catholic Church is suggesting to living Judaism that only a mutually respectful encounter between our deepest convictions—the Jewish conviction of the election of the people of Israel, and the Christian conviction that the God of Abraham, Moses, Isaiah, and Jeremiah revealed himself definitively in Jesus Christ—can exorcise the demons of past centuries, heal the wounds of prejudice, and create a different kind of future.

From the Catholic perspective, there is no encounter with Christ that is not an encounter with God's covenant with Israel and with the Jewish people, bearers of the promise of the Messiah. From the Catholic point of view, an ongoing and providential entanglement is built into the relationship between Christians and Jews.

Can faithful Jews share that conviction? Perhaps in a slightly different way. In the Jewish scheme of things, Christianity can never hold a place that is symmetrical with Judaism's place in Christian consciousness. That does not preclude faithful Jews from seeing, in Christianity, an expression of God's salvific purposes. That seems to be the direction in which the Jewish signatories of "Speak the Truth" are pointing. Cardinal Joseph Ratzinger pushes the suggestion just a bit further when he writes, "Israel may find it impossible to see Jesus as the Son of God as Christians do; but it is not impossible for [Israel] to see him as the Servant of God who carries the light of his God to the nations."[15]

Jesus, son of David, is he through whom Israel's God, the one true God, becomes the God of all the nations. Jesus, who said that he came to fulfill the Mosaic law (*Matthew* 5.17), is he through whom the Ten Commandments given to Israel become the moral patrimony of all "the nations." A serious exploration of these two readings of the Christian story and its ineradicable bond to Judaism would get the third millennium of the providential but often tortured entanglement of Catholics and Jews off to a promising start.

Who Is Saved? How?

"Vatican Claims Church Monopoly on Salvation," the headline in the *Washington Post* read. The Catholic Church teaches that a "person can achieve complete and eternal salvation only through Jesus Christ and the Roman Catholic Church," the listeners of National Public Radio were informed.[16] This kind of incendiary reporting in September 2000 on the Congregation for the Doctrine of the Faith's statement *Dominus Iesus* did not seem to portend a bright future for interreligious dialogue in the new century and millennium. In fact, however, the *Post* headline and the NPR report said more about the philosophical and theological confusions of the editors and the reporter in question than about the teaching of the Catholic Church. In the Catholic view of things, interreligious dialogue, like ecumenism, is far too important to let dissolve into another species of political correctness.

The Catholic Church's understanding of world religions and interreligious dialogue cannot be separated from the Catholic understanding of the mystery of the world's salvation. That understanding is quite specific and remarkably open-ended. Here it is, in summary form, according to Pope

John Paul II in the 1990 encyclical *Redemptoris Missio* [The Mission of the Redeemer]:

> While acknowledging that God loves all people and grants them the possibility of being saved (cf. *1 Timothy* 2.4), the Church believes that God has established Christ as the one mediator and that she herself has been established as the universal sacrament of salvation. . . . It is necessary to keep these two truths together, namely, the real possibility of salvation in Christ for all mankind and the necessity of the Church for salvation. Both these truths help us understand the *one mystery of salvation,* so that we can come to know God's mercy and our own responsibility. . . .
>
> The universality of salvation means that it is granted not only to those who explicitly believe in Christ and have entered the Church. Since salvation is offered to all, it must be made concretely available to all. But it is clear that today, as in the past, many people do not have an opportunity to come to know or accept the Gospel revelation or to enter the Church. . . . For such people salvation in Christ is accessible by virtue of a grace which, while having a mysterious relationship to the Church, does not make them formally part of the Church, but enlightens them in a way which is accommodated to their spiritual and material situation. This grace comes from Christ; it is the result of his sacrifice and is communicated by the Holy Spirit. It enables each person to attain salvation through his or her free cooperation.[17]

Does the Catholic Church teach that God wishes the salvation of all? Yes. Does the Catholic Church teach that that salvation was made possible for the world through the cross of Jesus Christ? Yes. Does the Catholic Church believe that there is salvation for those who do not know Christ? Yes. Does the Catholic Church believe that the salvation of those who do not know Christ is somehow made possible by Christ, whether or not those saved have ever heard of him? Yes. Does the Catholic Church believe that this puts all those saved in some relationship to the Catholic Church? Yes.

All of which may sound like an exercise in trying to have it both ways, or every which way. In truth, it is the Catholic Church's attempt to give doctrinal expression to the radical universality of God's love for the world and the radical specificity of God's self-revelation in Jesus Christ. The two go together. The Church cannot believe that Christ is anything other than the unique savior of the world; the Church cannot believe anything other than that God wills the salvation of all, whether or not they ever hear of Christ or the Catholic Church.

How the salvation of those who have not heard of Christ or believed in Christ is effected through Christ (and, because of Christ, through the Church) is something the Catholic Church frankly confesses that it does not understand. *Dominus Iesus* was widely attacked for its arrogance, and yet it was humble in confessing, with the Second Vatican Council, that the salvation comes to individual non-Christians in ways "known to [God] himself." *Dominus Iesus* also cited the Council in reminding Christians that if they are in a privileged position in the Church, that is not because of their merits but solely from the grace of Christ.[18] There is no room for arrogance here, although there is ample room for wonder—and for theological speculation. The Church does not know precisely how God saves the righteous who have not heard of or do not believe in Jesus Christ. The Church does know that this is what God does.

Why Bother with Missions?

If God wills the salvation of all, and if salvation is available to those who have never encountered Christ, then what is the point of Christian mission? In *Redemptoris Missio,* John Paul II identifies six reasons. By its very nature, the Church *is* a mission; to lose that missionary character would mean for the Church of the third millennium to break with the Church of the New Testament.[19] Christian mission is one way to fulfill Christ's commandment to love our neighbors. The "primary service" the Church does for the world is to preach Jesus Christ and offer others the possibility of coming to know him.[20] Christian mission is also a fulfillment of a Christian's duties to others, who have a right to know about Christ so that they might have the option of belief in Christ.[21]

Christian mission, the Pope goes on to suggest, strengthens Christian unity. Christian disunity is an obstacle to the proclamation of the Gospel, and a Church that takes its missionary responsibilities seriously must take ecumenism seriously, too.[22] Missionary commitment is the index of Christian faith. If Christians truly believe that God has saved them in Christ, then they will feel compelled to share Christ's Gospel with others. Mission, in other words, is what God demands of us. The salvation of others may not be imperiled by the failures of Christian mission; the salvation of Christians, whose failure to make Christ known is a failure to do God's will, may be.[23]

In the Church's mission to the nations, there must be complete respect for human freedom. The Church's missionary method must be the method of freedom: as John Paul wrote, underscoring the words for emphasis, "*The Church proposes; she imposes nothing*. . . . She respects individuals and cultures, and she honors the sanctuary of conscience."[24]

This "method of freedom" also shapes the Catholic approach to interreligious dialogue. Because it is a missionary Church convinced that all truths are related to the one Truth, who is God, the Catholic Church can encounter other world religions in genuine dialogue. The first question the Catholic Church asks in interreligious dialogue as well as in missionary activity is not "Why aren't you a Catholic?" but "What is the truth that guides your life?" Within a mutually respectful exploration of the truths of the human condition, the Church will explain itself and the truth it believes it carries in the world. That explanation is a proposal that takes the form of a question: "Does it seem to you that the truth as you have come to understand it might be more fully illuminated in the light of Christ?" Because the Catholic Church believes that all genuine truths in this world point toward the one great truth about the world—that the world has come from God and is destined for God—the Catholic Church can engage other world religions in the kind of dialogue that demonstrates, to skeptics and fanatics alike, that the encounter between convictions can lead to conversation, not conflict. In a twenty-first-century world that will be largely shaped by activist religious communities and movements, that is no small thing.

Finally, the Church's missionary mandate and the Church's commitment to interreligious dialogue reinforce the Church's commitment to religious freedom. In the Catholic view of things, religious freedom is the first of human rights, not because it has something to do with the Church making the most of its opportunities but because it is the right that arises from what is most distinctively human about human beings—their thirst for the truth of life. The Catholic defense of religious freedom is a defense of the religious freedom of everyone.

Different cultures and different world religions, John Paul II suggested to the United Nations in 1995, "are but different ways of facing the question of the meaning of human existence." At the heart of every culture is its distinctive approach to "the greatest of all mysteries: the mystery of God."[25] There can be no genuine respect for the human person without respect for the sanctuary of conscience in which that mystery and its truths are pondered. There can be no just state that does not recognize that sanctuary and that does not rigorously avoid abusing it. The fostering of a universal commitment to the priority of religious freedom should be one of the goals of interreligious dialogue.

The Church's insistence on its missionary character and the Church's commitment to a truth-based interreligious dialogue are part of the Church's answer to those who claim that any encounter between ultimate convictions necessarily leads to violent conflict. State-enforced secularism is a threat to civil peace, just as coercive religion can be. To coercive secularists and coercive religious communities, the Catholic Church says: The people most likely to respect human rights, defend religious freedom, and build a human community of dialogue, not confrontation, are the people who believe that it is God's will that they respect the convictions of neighbors who have different convictions about God.

9

Is Catholicism Safe for Democracy?

Living Freedom for Excellence in Public

An eminent historian, Arthur M. Schlesinger, Sr., once said that "the deepest bias in the history of the American people" is the suspicion that the Catholic Church is not quite safe for democracy. However one ranks the abiding prejudices in the American national psyche, mistrust of Catholicism's impact on democracy has a long and distinguished pedigree.

Schoolchildren in seventeenth-century New England were taught to sing, "Abhor that arrant Whore of Rome, / And all her blasphemies, / And drink not of her cursèd cup, / Obey not her decrees." John Adams, writing to Abigail from the Continental Congress in Philadelphia in 1774, described his visit to "the Romish chapel" waspishly:

> The entertainment was to me most awful and affecting: the poor wretches fingering their beads, chanting Latin, not a

> word of which they understood . . . their holy water; their crossing themselves perpetually; their bowing to the name of Jesus whenever they heard it; their bowings, kneelings, and genuflections before the altar. . . . Here is everything which can lay hold of the eye, ear, and imagination—everything which can charm and bewitch the simple and ignorant. I wonder how Luther ever broke the spell.

One of the best-selling books in America in the decades before the Civil War was a mendacious and lurid potboiler entitled *Maria Monk's Awful Disclosures of the Hotel Dieu Nunnery in Montreal,* which purported to reveal sexual shenanigans in a convent. Mark Twain, a man with a refreshingly skeptical view of most received wisdom, once confessed frankly that "I have been educated to enmity toward everything that is Catholic." Francis Parkman's epic seven-volume study, *France and England in North America,* organizes two hundred years of history through the prism of a great struggle between the party of liberty (Protestant England) and the party of authoritarianism (Catholic France).

From the colonial period through the mid-twentieth century, the fear that Catholicism was dangerous to American liberties reflected ancient religious and ethnic prejudices. After World War II, those who questioned Catholicism's compatibility with democracy took a different tack. In his 1949 bestseller, *American Freedom and Catholic Power,* Paul Blanshard argued that the United States had a "Catholic problem." The Catholic Church, Blanshard wrote, was an "undemocratic system of alien control" in which laypeople were chained by the "absolute rule of the clergy." A year later, in *Communism,*

Democracy, and Catholic Power, Blanshard compared the "two alien and undemocratic centers," Moscow and Rome, noting the alleged parallels between their "structure of power," their "management of truth," their "thought control," and their "strategy of penetration." As Blanshard's ablest Catholic critic, Father John Courtney Murray, S.J., wrote in response to these canards, this was not the old Protestant-based anti-Catholic nativism, convinced that only native-born Protestants could be true Americans; this was a "new nativism," determined to enforce its view that democracy could not coexist with transcendent moral norms.

For the new nativism, which could also be called radical secularism, Catholicism was the largest institutional obstacle to a great political project: making the United States a country in which religiously grounded values and arguments have no place in public life. That project continues to this day. The same year the Berlin Wall fell, the editors of the *New York Times* warned the Catholic bishops of the United States that a too-vigorous exercise of their teaching office in addressing the abortion issue might destroy the "truce of tolerance" that permitted Catholics to be citizens of a country with a non-Catholic majority. A year later, the editorial page editor of the *Philadelphia Inquirer* wrote that "the Roman Catholic Church . . . is quite literally an *un-American* institution." During a Pennsylvania debate on school choice in the 1990s, a local teachers' union president told his school board that "the enemy to public education in the state of Pennsylvania is the Catholic Church. If the Catholic Church were to cease to exist and disappear today, it would be better for all of us."

There is a profound irony here. In the eighteenth and

nineteenth centuries, anti-Catholic bigots in America could at least appeal to official Roman skepticism about that new political arrangement called "democracy." During the past thirty years, though, the Catholic Church has been perhaps the world's foremost institutional promoter of the democratic project.

As even Mikhail Gorbachev frankly concedes, Pope John Paul II and the Catholic resistance in east central Europe played large roles in the collapse of European communism and the nonviolent transition to democracy in the countries of the old Warsaw Pact. The bishops of the Philippines urged Catholic priests, religious, and laity to support the 1985–86 People Power revolution against the Marcos dictatorship, and the people took to the streets by the hundreds of thousands to restore democracy to their country. Throughout Latin America, the Catholic Church was a major force in the democratic transitions of the 1980s and 1990s; the beginning of the end of the Pinochet dictatorship in Chile, for example, can be traced to Pope John Paul II's pilgrimage to that country in 1987. The Church has even played a significant role in the democratic transformation of a traditionally non-Christian country, South Korea.

In the face of this overwhelming evidence, the charge that the Catholic Church is inherently antidemocratic is ignorant as well as malicious. And yet it continues. Why? Because it is a stalking-horse for another argument.

The real issue being engaged today is not whether Catholicism is safe for democracy, but "What kind of democracy?" The contemporary critics of the Church are, in many cases, the linear descendants of Paul Blanshard and his new secular nativism, and the Catholic Church is the primary institutional obstacle to the project of enforcing a thoroughly secularized public life in the United States. In that project's view of the democratic future, there is no place in democratic debate for the assertion of unchanging, binding moral truths—except, of course, for the "absolute truth" that there are no absolute moral truths. Binding moral truths, according to the secularists, are incompatible with democracy because moral truth cannot bind us and free us at the same time.

That was not, of course, the view of the American Founders, who pledged their "lives, liberties, and sacred honor" to a democracy built on "self-evident" moral truths about life, liberty, and the pursuit of happiness. Convictions about the enduring nature of those self-evident truths continue to animate the lives of millions of Americans of every religious persuasion and none. So the debate will continue—with, one hopes, a more accurate understanding of what is really at stake.

What will the Catholic Church bring to that debate? What does the Catholic Church believe and teach about democracy?

MAKING DEMOCRATS

Flying to South America in 1987, Pope John Paul II was asked by a reporter whether he would press the Pinochet regime to return Chile to democracy. The Pope's answer was instructive: "I am not the evangelizer of democracy, I am the evangelizer of the Gospel. To the Gospel message, of course, belongs all the problems of human rights, and if democracy means human rights then it also belongs to the message of the Church."[1]

The sequence here was not accidental, and it demonstrates how several themes explored previously shape the contemporary Catholic view of democracy.

Evangelism comes first, because the proclamation of God's passionate love for the world is what the Church is for. The Gospel, however, is not a private matter. The Gospel has public implications, because defending the inalienable dignity and infinite value built into human beings by their Creator is a public matter. One way the Gospel has public effects is through the formation of cultures: a culture inspired by a Christian view of the human person will affirm certain kinds of politics as compatible with the dignity of men and women, and it will reject others for their incompatibility with that dignity. The Church is not in the business of designing or running governments; the Church is in the business of forming the kind of people who can design and run governments in which freedom leads to genuine human flourishing. From evangelism to culture formation to political change: that is the public strategy of the Catholic Church in the twenty-first century, a strategy effectively deployed in the last decades of the twentieth century by Pope John Paul II.

To put it another way, the Catholic Church thinks about democracy through the prism of its convictions about the nature of human beings, their hunger for goodness, and their yearning for a freedom that truly liberates. Those convictions about who we are lead to certain further convictions about politics, that essential human activity. In the Catholic view of the contemporary political order, democracy is not just a set of electoral, legislative, judicial, and executive institutions and procedures. Democracy is a way of public life, a way of being a political community. That way of life is characterized by equality before the law, participation in decision making, civility, a passion for justice, and a commitment to both individual liberty and the common good. The democratic way of life makes the procedures and institutions of democracy—elections, legislatures, courts, and so forth—possible.

Democracy is not, in other words, a machine that will run by itself. The Catholic Church has been thinking about governance and public life for a long time. On the basis of the experience of centuries, the Church is convinced that it takes a certain kind of people to make democracy work. It takes people who have made their own the values, the moral truths, that teach us to be civil, tolerant, respectful—in a word, democratic.

The institutions of democracy demand a critical mass of democrats in a society. That critical mass—what political theorists call "civil society"—is formed by moral convictions: about rights and duties, about the proper relationship between those who govern and those who are governed, about the rule of law and the meaning of justice. Those convictions do not come to us easily. Every two-year-old is, by nature, a tyrant. All those two-year-olds have to be taught to be democrats. Parents do that; neighbors and relatives and friends do that. And the Catholic Church does that, by teaching young and old alike the dignity of the human person.

The Foundations of the House of Freedom

To be sure, this understanding of democracy is in sharp conflict with the idea that democracies must be value-neutral. That notion, widespread in western Europe, North America, Australia, and New Zealand, was also gaining acceptance in some of the new democracies of east central Europe in the early 1990s. In his 1991 encyclical, *Centesimus Annus* [The Hundredth Year], Pope John Paul II, an architect of the revolution of freedom in that part of the world, challenged democracies old and new to a richer, nobler concept of the democratic experiment. After repeating the Church's appreciation of democracy for fostering participation in public life, public service, and the resolution of conflict through law rather than violence, the Pope directly addressed the question of democracy's cultural foundations:

> Authentic democracy is possible only in a state ruled by law, and on the basis of a correct concept of the human person. . . . Nowadays there is a tendency to claim that agnosticism and skeptical relativism are the philosophy and the basic attitude which correspond to democratic forms of political life. Those who are convinced that they know the truth and firmly adhere to it are considered unreliable from a democratic point of view, since they do not accept that truth is determined by the majority, or that it is subject to variation according to different political trends. [But] . . . if there is no ultimate truth to guide and direct political activity, then ideas and convictions can easily be manipulated for

> reasons of power. As history demonstrates, a democracy without values easily turns into open or thinly disguised totalitarianism.[2]

The last word stung. Was the Pope suggesting that the democracies, which had twice defeated twentieth-century totalitarianisms, risked becoming what they had poured out lives and treasure to oppose? That was, in fact, what the Pope was suggesting, but with a crucial difference. John Paul did not fear a new outbreak of fascism, Nazism, or communism; these, he knew, were spent political creeds. The present danger was more subtle.

A new kind of tyranny, all the more dangerous because it wasn't as visible as a Nazi tank or a Soviet missile, was encoded within the notion that democracy is a value-neutral machine that can run by itself—a machine that can do politics and public policy and legislating and judging and all the rest of it without transcendent moral reference points. The danger was a new tyranny of raw power. If a democracy banned any consideration of binding moral norms as a horizon for its public life, on the grounds that moral truth was either illusory or sectarian, then conflicts within that democracy could be resolved only by resort to force.

One group, exercising its will through legislation, judicial fiat, or more coercive means, would impose its judgment on everyone else. The losers, in turn, would think, correctly, that their rights had been violated. The net result would be the breakdown of democratic political community—the civil society that makes democratic self-government possible. Chaos, leading to some form of tyranny, would certainly follow. A democracy without values is self-cannibalizing. Freedom, absent moral truth, becomes its own worst enemy.

That was what John Paul meant by democracies running the risk of becoming "thinly disguised totalitarianisms." The Pope, who knew the history of the twentieth century in his bones, knew all about the great democratic failure of his time, which was the failure of the Weimar Republic in post–World War I Germany. The Weimar Republic had a beautifully crafted set of democratic institutions and a constitution drafted in part by one of the great social theorists of the century, Max Weber. Yet that splendid edifice of institutions rested on wholly inadequate moral and cultural foundations. When times got hard, the foundations proved incapable of supporting the structure, the whole thing collapsed—and the result was a civilized people's embrace of tyranny. That, John Paul was suggesting, was a lesson for everyone.

On the other side of these papal warnings was a different kind of proposal. Think, John Paul II suggested, of all the important things that a sense of transcendent moral truth does for a democracy.

Take, for example, the question of equality. The equality of everyone before the law and the political equality of all citizens are bedrock democratic principles. How do we convince the next generation (or ourselves, for that matter) that those principles make sense in a world where people are clearly unequal in intelligence, beauty, wealth, and skill? Recognizing that everyone is equal before the demands of the moral law, John Paul suggests, is the sturdiest possible foundation on which to sustain our commitments to democratic legal and political equality.[3] If no one gets a pass from the obligations laid down by the moral law, then we really are equal in a very basic, and very human, way.

Then there is the question of civil society. Democracies,

which tend to be boisterous and contentious, need what French philosopher Jacques Maritain once called "civic friendship" in order to flourish amid endless political, social, and legal conflicts. If all the relationships in a democracy are merely contractual—if the only thing that binds me to my fellow citizens is my right to sue them and theirs to sue me—democracy will crumble, or choke to death on litigation. Some deeper, nobler bond is needed. Forging those bonds of civil friendship, John Paul suggests, is easier when we see in our neighbors a common obligation to commonly recognized moral truths—when we see our neighbors as fellow citizens engaged in the same great project of building goodness and justice with the tools of freedom.[4]

Running through this analysis is a deep Catholic conviction that democracies need to live freedom for excellence if the democratic experiment is to prosper. Virtues are a serious issue for democracies. In an absolute monarchy, a virtuous king can be sufficient to ensure justice and good government. Democracies need a critical mass of virtuous citizens if justice is to be done—if the rights of others, as well as our own rights, are to be cherished and respected. How can a democracy that resolutely bars transcendent moral norms from public life develop the strength that comes from civic virtue? Would segregation have been defeated in the United States if America's religious communities had not taken an assertive public role in shaping consciences and demanding legal change? The questions, once asked, seem to answer themselves: democracy is not a machine that can run by itself.

In the Catholic view of things, democracy is like a house. A democracy must be built on a firm foundation, like any house.

That foundation is not political or legal: it is cultural. A democratic political community is built on, and sustained by, a democratic culture.

The foundations of the house of freedom are the virtues of the people, brought into public life so that they shape a democratic culture and, ultimately, a democratic government. When those virtues and the moral truths that shape them are ruled out-of-bounds in public life, the foundations of the house of freedom are weakened. If they crack, the future of the house is threatened—not by external enemies but by an internal deficit of virtue.

That is why, in the Catholic view, "value-neutral democracy" is a contradiction in terms. And that is why the Catholic Church insists that religiously informed moral truths have a place in public life. The issue here is not the Church's desire to be a partisan political player. The issue is securing the foundations of the house of freedom.

All of which suggests that, in this matter of Catholicism and democracy, the question is no longer whether Catholicism can accept democracy. The question is whether democracies that do not attend seriously to the security and strength of their moral and cultural foundations can long endure.

The Life Issues: Abortion and Euthanasia

No issue of the Catholic Church's public engagement with democratic politics has been more bitterly contested than abortion. Times beyond counting, before and after the

U.S. Supreme Court federalized the issue in *Roe v. Wade* (1973), the Catholic Church has been accused of trying to force its sectarian moral judgments on a pluralistic nation. (Why the Catholic Church's defense of the laws of forty-some states prior to *Roe v. Wade* should be considered a sectarian matter is an interesting question; one somehow doubts that Catholic moral theology deeply influenced the pre-*Roe* abortion laws of Utah or Alabama.) In any event, the Catholic Church has never understood itself to be engaged in a sectarian argument about abortion. It has understood itself to be defending the dignity of human life, on publicly accessible moral grounds, on an issue it believes is at the very center of the quest to secure the foundations of the house of freedom.

Catholic teaching on abortion is based on what the Church understands to be a classic and invariable principle of morality: "The direct and voluntary killing of an innocent human being is always gravely immoral."[5] We can know this by reason; men and women of faith also know it from revelation. "Thou shalt not kill" (more accurately, "You shall do no murder") is not a moral injunction for Jews and Christians only; it is a universal moral norm, inscribed on the human heart, recognized by every ethical system, religious or philosophical, and codified in every state's civil law. No combination of intentions or consequences can ever justify the taking of an innocent human life.

That the unborn child is a human being from the moment of conception is a fact that we know by logic and biological evidence. Nothing that will be a human being is ever anything other than a human being; nothing that is not a human being will ever become a human being. Those logical truths are amply confirmed by modern science, which has demonstrated beyond dispute that every human being, from the moment of conception, is a unique (and uniquely human) genetic package. Absent natural disaster or lethal intervention, the product of human conception will be what every sane person recognizes as a human being; it will not be a goldfish or a golden retriever.[6] As to the claim that, in the early stages of pregnancy, what the Church calls a "human being" is really only a clump of cells (an argument made by a nationally syndicated columnist during a recent debate over the killing of embryos and "pre-embryos" for medical research), the Church can only respond that that "clump of cells" is precisely what the columnist looked like at that stage of his life—and precisely what all his readers looked like at that stage of theirs.

The Church fully recognizes that unwanted and unplanned pregnancy can be a profoundly wrenching, frightening experience. Far more than those abortion advocates and providers who suggest that terminating a pregnancy is of little more consequence than having a tonsillectomy, the Church understands that unwanted pregnancy is a deeply traumatic experience in which a woman feels that her entire life has been entrapped. The Church also understands that trying to escape that entrapment through abortion can be emotionally and spiritually shattering. That is why the Church supports a vast network of crisis pregnancy centers; that is why numerous Catholic bishops have told women caught in the dilemma of unwanted pregnancy that the Church will support them financially and medically if they choose to carry their child to term, and will then help arrange either adoption or employment, if the mother decides to keep her child; that is why the Church established Project Rachel, a counseling service for women suffering postabortion trauma. The Catholic Church has not simply inveighed against abortion; it has put its personnel and its resources at the service of women in crisis.

In the Catholic view of things, abortion is a justice issue, not an issue of sexual morality. The commandment involved here is the injunction against murder, not the injunction against sexual sin. The dilemma of unwanted pregnancy inevitably and inescapably involves two lives, two human beings. The Catholic Church tries to be of service to both, and tries to defend the legitimate rights of both. But the Church also insists that it is a question of both.

That is why, for the Catholic Church, abortion is an issue with public consequences. It is not a private choice. It is not a matter of sectarian morality. The defense of the inalienable right to life of the unborn is a civil rights issue—arguably the greatest civil rights issue of our time. If the state claims the right to declare an entire class of human beings—the unborn—outside the boundaries of legal protection, then no one is safe. A society that permits lethal violence as a means of resolving a personal dilemma is not a society fully governed by the rule of law; it is a society governed in crucial respects by the rule of raw, unchecked power. If the legal principle that the strong have the right to declare the weak outside the boundaries of the community of common protection is firmly established, all those whom the strong might someday declare unfit, unproductive, troublesome, or inconvenient are in peril.

Securing the right to life of the unborn means changing contemporary culture as well as reforming the laws. That is why many Catholic leaders (and some politicians) have adopted Father Richard John Neuhaus's twofold definition of the pro-life goal: a society in which every child is protected in law and welcomed in life. Service to women in crisis is one essential complement to the Church's public argument for legal protection of the unborn. The creation of a sexually responsible society, in which women are not treated as the discardable objects of transitory male pleasure, left to solve their "problem" on their own, is another essential part of the Catholic pro-life agenda.

Because this is a civil rights issue, the Catholic Church has always tried to make its argument in favor of the legal protection of the unborn in explicitly public terms. The statements by the bishops of the United States on abortion can be engaged and debated by anyone willing to take an argument seriously. So have been many of the statements of Pope John Paul II on this issue. Receiving the credentials of U.S. ambassador Corinne C. Boggs in 1997, the Pope put his case in unmistakably public, and unmistakably democratic, terms:

> No expression of today's [American] commitment to liberty and justice for all can be more basic than the protection afforded to those in society who are most vulnerable. The United States of America was founded on the conviction that an inalienable right to life was a self-evident moral truth, fidelity to which was a primary criterion of social justice. The moral history of your country is the story of your people's efforts to widen the circle of inclusion in society, so that all Americans might enjoy the protection of law, participate in the responsibilities of citizenship, and have the opportunity to make a contribution to the common good. Whenever a certain category of people—the unborn, or the

> sick and old—are excluded from that protection, a deadly anarchy subverts the original understanding of justice. The credibility of the United States will depend more and more on its promotion of a genuine culture of life, and on a renewed commitment to building a world in which the weakest and most vulnerable are welcomed and protected.[7]

A parallel set of moral judgments shapes Catholic thinking about euthanasia. The legalization of physician-assisted suicide damages the moral foundations of the house of freedom just as abortion does. By putting the weak and vulnerable outside the boundaries of legal protection, the weak and the vulnerable are put at risk. So is everyone else. And the basic democratic principle of "liberty and justice for all" is violated. The Church has also read the unmistakable evidence, from the Netherlands and elsewhere, that where euthanasia is permitted it is soon expected, even required, with or without a patient's consent. As for end-of-life care, the Church does not demand the continuation of "medical procedures that are burdensome, dangerous, extraordinary, or disproportionate to the expected outcome"; but it does not consider food and water "extraordinary" measures.[8] And it asks what is happening to a people who come to think of these basic forms of human caring as extraordinary.

To those who believe that abortion and euthanasia contribute to human dignity, the Catholic Church proposes, "We need to talk about the meaning of 'dignity'—and why anything that denies the inalienability of the right to life is an assault on human dignity, no matter how well intentioned."

To those who deem abortion and euthanasia relatively meaningless as issues of public policy because they involve "private" choices, the Church proposes two questions: "Do you really think it a 'private choice' when another human being is involved? Do you think that allowing the state to legitimate lethal violence as a way to resolve personal problems, no matter how grievous, is a good thing in itself, and for democracy?"

To those who say that choice in these matters is an essential component of freedom, the Church proposes a new conversation: "We must talk about freedom for excellence. We must explore, together, our conviction that freedom linked to truth and fulfilled in goodness is the only freedom that is truly human freedom—and the only freedom that can sustain democracy."

The Church proposes; she imposes nothing. The Church seeks to be the teacher of the nations, not the ruler of nations. On these questions she will propose, and propose, and then propose some more. The Catholic commitment to human dignity, and the Catholic commitment to democracy, demand it.

10

What Will Become of Us?

Saints and the Human Future

Because the twentieth century was a century of great fears, it produced a brilliant literature of antiutopias, chilling portraits of a dehumanized future, the roots of which a keen-eyed novelist could detect here and now. Written at a time when it seemed as if totalitarianism might seize control of the world, George Orwell's *1984* was one such gripping probe around the corner of history. As the twenty-first century opens, though, it seems that Aldous Huxley had a clearer view than Orwell of the long-term threat to human freedom.

Written a quarter century before the unraveling of DNA, Huxley's *Brave New World* was astonishingly prescient about the possibility that biotechnology and eugenics could eventually remanufacture the human condition by manufacturing human beings. To this scientific foresight, Huxley added a philosophical, even spiritual intuition about the distortion of ideas and values that would make the brave new world seem desirable, rational, humane.

In Huxley's novel, Mustapha Mond is one of the World Controllers whose responsibilities include making sure that heretical ideas don't get loose to roil the placid waters of the brave new world, which is a world without significant conflicts. One day, Mustapha Mond receives a paper by Bernard Marx, a scientist whose prenatal conditioning didn't quite take and who has an inquiring and sometimes cranky mind. The World Controller, bred to genius, admires Marx's mathematical and speculative skills. But Mustapha Mond finally decides that the paper is not to be published, that Bernard Marx is to be kept under supervision, and that he may have to be transferred to a remote island research station. Why?

Because his paper suggested that there might be purpose in the world and in human lives. And that, Mustapha Mond understood, was the one idea that could never be let loose again:

> [O]nce you began admitting explanations in terms of purpose—well, you didn't know what the results would be. It was the sort of idea that might easily decondition the more unsettled minds among the higher castes—make them lose their faith in happiness as the Sovereign Good and take to believing, instead, that the goal was somewhere beyond, somewhere outside the present human sphere; that the purpose of life was not the maintenance of well-being, but some intensification and refinement of consciousness, some enlargement of knowledge. Which was, the Controller reflected, quite possibly true. But not, in the present circumstances, admissible. He picked up his pen again, and

> under the words *"Not to be published,"* drew a second line, thicker and blacker than the first.[1]

Huxley's brave new world is not miserably oppressive, like the jackbooted world of *1984;* Huxley's is a happy antiutopia. But it is a world of stunted humanity: a world of souls without longing, without passion, without sacrifice, without suffering, without surprises or desire—in a word, a world without love. What made such a world seem humane to its creators? The conviction that made the brave new world possible was the conviction that the world and the human beings who inhabit it are essentially purposeless. There is no goal to be discerned in the physical world or in our lives. The humane thing to do, if you were among those enlightened enough to see this, was to create a world without striving—a world in which immediate physical and psychic gratification was always available in the form of a chemical or sexual substitute for those rumors of angels that had bewitched humanity for millennia.

What Aldous Huxley foresaw as scientific possibility is now, in the main, scientific fact. When the British government establishes a Human Fertilisation and Embryology Authority, so reminiscent of Huxley's Central London Hatchery and Conditioning Centre, we are clearly living in the antechamber of the brave new world already. The question is whether humanity in the twenty-first century will have the wit and the will to bend the new genetics and the new biotechnologies to ends that enhance genuine human freedom and happiness.

The question "What will become of us?" has haunted humankind for centuries. If purposelessness and randomness really do define the world and us, then one possible answer to that perennial question and the fear embedded in it is the happy dehumanization of Huxley's novel. Within decades, perhaps sooner, humankind will have the technological means to travel down that road. We can freely choose to abandon our freedom and put our faith in mundane happiness as "the Sovereign Good." We can also see, in *Brave New World,* where that will lead.

What does the Catholic Church and the Catholic vision of things have to say about the human future? "What will become of us?" is a question for Christians, too—and fittingly enough, because it was the cry of Jesus from the cross: "My God, my God, why have you forsaken me?" (*Matthew* 27.46). Catholics believe that God's ultimate answer to Christ's question, and ours, was given in the resurrection. But what does that say about us *now*? God's promise of eternal beatitude can seem a long way off, no matter how old we are. What is to become of us between now and then?

The answer in brief: we must become saints.

St. Everyone

Shortly after publishing his novel *Helena,* in which he retold the story of the emperor Constantine's mother and her quest for the true cross, Evelyn Waugh received a congratulatory note from a friend, the poet John Betjeman. Betjeman complimented Waugh on the book but wrote that "Helena doesn't seem like a saint." Waugh, who had tried for years to entice the devoutly Anglican Betjeman into the Catholic

Church, replied with a brief catechesis on the Catholic understanding of saints:

> Saints are simply souls in heaven. Some people have been so sensationally holy in life that we know they went straight to heaven and so put them in the [liturgical] calendar. We all have to become saints before we get to heaven. . . . And each individual has his own peculiar form of sanctity which he must achieve or perish. It is no good my saying, "I wish I were like Joan of Arc or St. John of the Cross." I can only be St. Evelyn Waugh—after God knows what experiences in purgatory.
>
> I liked Helena's sanctity because it is in contrast to all that moderns think of as sanctity. She wasn't thrown to the lions, she wasn't a contemplative, she wasn't poor and hungry, she didn't look like an El Greco. She just discovered what it was God had chosen for her to do and did it.[2]

Waugh's letter to Betjeman sums up two facets of the Catholic view of who we are and what we must become. The first is that sainthood is everyone's destiny—sainthood is everyone's purpose. In a world that often imagines itself purposeless, Catholicism proposes a dramatic, transcendent purpose for every human life: the life of a saint. The second, equally striking aspect of the Catholic view of saints is that sainthood is not generic, but quite specific. Becoming a saint means living out a unique vocation, a distinctive role in the cosmic drama that can be filled by no one else. Discerning that vocation, giving oneself to it, and then dying in it is the drama of the Christian life as the Catholic Church understands it.

The drama points, at every juncture, toward the infinite. In becoming the saints we are made to be, we become the kind of people who can live with God forever.

Albert Camus, the French existentialist writer and philosopher who had a tortured relationship to Catholicism, once created a memorable dialogue about human fulfillment. Camus rejected the fashionable despair of purposelessness he found in the existentialism of Jean-Paul Sartre. At the same time, in his fiction, Camus tried to articulate a philosophy of existence that, while stoically denying any ultimate transcendence, still underscored the intense drama of the human condition here and now. Thus, when one of Camus's characters says that he is interested in being a saint, his interlocutor replies that he is interested in being a man—to which the first character responds that they're both interested in the same thing, but his friend is more ambitious.

It's a nice turn of phrase, but it may be too clever by half. In the Catholic view of things, the two go together. The way we grow into our humanity is to grow into the saints we are meant to be—the saints we must be as our personal drama is fit into the cosmic drama of creation, redemption, and sanctification in which we are playing. Becoming a saint means emptying ourselves of ourselves in order to fill ourselves with vocational passion. Growing into sainthood, like falling in love, is a mysterious process in which the gift of ourselves comes back to us multiplied. Living the Law of the Gift in the singular way that God has in mind for each of us is the way we are amplified and enriched in the very process of being emptied.

That, the Catholic Church believes, is everyone's vocation.

Prime Numbers, and the Rest of Us

Reading the lives of the saints used to be a standard part of Catholic devotional life. It's a practice that seems to have fallen out of favor in recent decades, although a quick survey of recent publishers' catalogues suggests that lives of the saints are making a comeback. As well they might. Discovering the saints officially recognized by the Church is a powerful tool for discerning ways to grow into the unique sainthood to which each Christian is called.

Who are these officially recognized saints? Clarifying some misunderstandings about them helps bring their lives and their meaning into clearer focus—and suggests what they have to do with us.

The Catholic Church doesn't "make" saints, and neither does the Pope. Through the teaching authority of the Bishop of Rome, acting on the counsel of his advisers, the Church recognizes the saints that God has made. This process of saint making, or saint recognizing, used to be highly legalistic and included such picaresque characters as the "devil's advocate," a postmortem prosecuting attorney whose job it was to challenge claims to sanctity on the assumption that all candidates were not saint material until proven so. Pope John Paul II changed all this in 1983, turning the process into something far more akin to a doctoral seminar in history than a court trial.

One result of the changed process has been the unprecedented number of saints John Paul II has canonized (447 as of October 2000) and the even larger number of men and women he has beatified, or declared "blessed"—the last step toward officially recognized sainthood (994 as of October 2000). These canonizations and beatifications—of a Sudanese slave girl and a Milanese bon vivant of the Roaring Twenties; priests, nuns, and laity martyred during the French Revolution, the Cristero rebellion in Mexico, the Spanish Civil War, and the Second World War; a Philadelphia heiress and a Roman pediatrician who sacrificed her own life to save her unborn child; journalists and mystics; Vietnamese, Koreans, Chinese, a Nigerian, a Gypsy, and sundry indigenous peoples, as well as Europeans from the Old and New Worlds; an assertive Australian nun of Scottish extraction who was once excommunicated by her irascible Irish bishop and a brilliant philosopher whose life as a Carmelite nun ended in the gas chambers of Auschwitz—are remarkable for the diversity of their biographies. Saints are not just people from the distant past whom we remember once a year on their liturgical feast day. John Paul II's canonizations and beatifications are a powerful reminder that saints are all around us, in virtually every imaginable venue of life. Sanctity is not just for the sanctuary on Sunday. Sanctity is a real possibility for everyone, all the time and everywhere.

Canonizing Bernadette Soubirous, the visionary of Lourdes, in 1933, Pope Pius XI said that saints were like telescopes that let us see stars invisible to the naked eye. Saints help us see truths and possibilities amid the quotidian realities of life. Theologian Hans Urs von Balthasar subdivides the saints into two basic types. Some saints have an entirely singular vocation, demonstrating a previously unknown, unexplored, or underappreciated facet of God's plan for the Church and the world. These are the saints Balthasar calls "God's prime numbers"; St. Francis of Assisi, whose radical embrace of poverty and nature must have made him seem like a man from another planet in medieval Italy, is a paradigm of the type. Other saints emerge more organically, as exemplars of recognized vocations: mothers and fathers, consecrated religious and clergy, artists and scholars who have lived their lives in holy, if not necessarily pathbreaking, ways. The Church recognizes that in this more typical kind of vocational self-giving, sanctity is also a real possibility.

Among the saints, both the prime numbers and the exemplars help the rest of us respond to our vocational call to sainthood. The prime numbers remind us that there are always new dimensions to sanctity to be discovered, and they warn the institutional Church about the dangers of complacency. The exemplars teach us that even those less fiercely touched by God's call can, through God's grace, become fitted for a life of eternal beatitude.

Then there are the martyrs. Pope John Paul II has reminded the Church for more than twenty years that the martyr is the Christian ideal. The martyr is a witness whose life coincides completely with the truth by being given entirely to the truth in self-sacrificing love. Martyrdom, too, is all around us. Those who think of martyrs as people to whom grisly things happened in the Roman Coliseum two millennia ago should reflect on the fact that the twentieth century was the greatest century of martyrdom in Christian history.[3] More Christians gave their lives for their faith in the twentieth century than in the previous nineteen centuries of Christian history combined.

The ubiquity of contemporary martyrdom—27 million, by one reliable estimate—is a story of remarkable personal heroism. In the many brutal hearts of darkness that scarred the twentieth century, the light still shone forth. The vast numbers of modern martyrs are also a powerful response to those who suggest that modernity can't afford the luxury of a sense of purpose in life. That some 27 million men and women from all over the world saw a purpose in life that transcended life here and now tells us something very important about the human condition at the turn of a new millennium. It tells us that the rumors of angels are still being heard, even when their message is a call to the ultimate gift of self, the gift of one's life in martyrdom.

Miracles and Modernity

Miracles can seem desperately old-fashioned, even superstitious, in a world that has grown accustomed to heart transplants, in utero surgeries to remedy birth defects, instant communications, and space travel. Yet the Catholic Church still insists that validating miracles, attributed to the intercession of a candidate for sainthood, are necessary for beatification and canonization (or in the case of martyrs, who can be beatified without a confirming miracle, for canonization). The Church defines a miracle as "a sign or wonder, such as a healing or control of nature, which can only be attributed to divine power."[4] In the process of recognizing saints, alleged miracles must be examined by a scientific panel. A cure is accepted as miraculous only if current medical science can provide no other explanation for it. Miracles, in this sense, are an ecclesiastical insurance policy—God's confirmation that the Church has not made a serious error in proposing a candidate for sainthood.

There is another connection between the miraculous and the saints, one that touches those who will never experience the wonder of a confirmed miraculous cure. In the Gospels, Jesus' healing miracles are not demonstrations of power designed to induce or seduce faith; Jesus' cures are the results of faith. After a leper professes his faith in the power of Jesus, Jesus cures him (*Matthew* 8.2–3); after the centurion declares his unworthiness that Jesus should enter his house, his servant is cured (*Matthew* 8.5–13); after a sick woman confesses her faith in him, Jesus cures her hemorrhage and tells her that her faith has saved her (*Matthew* 9.20–22). These miracles are signs illustrating Jesus' great message that the Kingdom of God is right here, breaking into the world, among us.

We can describe the inexplicable today as "phenomena that go beyond the norms." Or we can describe the inexplicable as the miraculous. When the Catholic Church describes an inexplicable cure as a miracle in the process of recognizing a saint, it is proposing, once again, that the extraordinary lies just on the far side of the ordinary in this sacramentally configured world. We know that the Earth is round, but we often live as if the world were flat. Miracles, and the saints through whom miracles are worked, are challenges to the flatness of the world.

Miracles and saints are also an invitation to a deeper generosity, a more humane engagement with those who share this world with us. The basilica at Lourdes is one of the most popular pilgrimage sites in the world. The International Medical Commission of Lourdes has confirmed numerous scientifically inexplicable cures of cancer, tuberculosis, and blindness there. Yet those who have been to Lourdes know that the miracles of Lourdes go beyond physical cures. Caught up in the intense prayerfulness and remarkable peace of the place, the strong and healthy find themselves transformed from tourists into pilgrims, helping the weak and infirm into the waters that flow from the once-hidden spring the Virgin Mary showed to Bernadette Soubirous. The spirits of all are calmed and cured, even if bodies remain ill. The world of suffering is transformed into a world of peace at Lourdes, where we learn that the extraordinary breaks into the ordinary in acts of human solidarity and kindness, as well as in ways that are scientifically inexplicable.

That is what saints and miracles do for us. They help make us into the kind of people we are meant to be.

A Choice of Worlds

In his apostolic letter closing the Great Jubilee of 2000, Pope John Paul II returned once again to the teaching of the Second Vatican Council on the universal call to holiness. The Council stressed the vocation to sanctity, the Pope writes, not just to "embellish" the idea of the Church with "a kind of spiritual veneer" but to remind us that holiness is what the Church is *for.* In baptism, Christians are called beyond mediocrity, beyond relativism, beyond a shallow "spirituality." As the Pope puts it, when the Church in its baptismal rite asks adult converts, or the parents and sponsors of infants, "Do you wish baptism?" the Church is asking, "Do you wish to become holy?" This means putting before all the baptized "the radical nature of the Sermon on the Mount: 'Be perfect as your heavenly Father is perfect' (*Matthew* 5.48)."[5]

The brave new world tells us that we ought to settle for a middling happiness in a life free of trouble. Catholicism tells us not only that we are capable of greatness but that greatness is demanded of us.

The brave new world is a world of rationally organized self-indulgence. The world of the saints is a world of radical, extravagant self-giving.

The brave new world is flat, painless, essentially carefree. The world of the saints is always craggy and sometimes painful; it includes dark nights of the soul as well as moments of ecstatic love.

Which is the more human world?

Which is the more liberated world?

Which is the world on which you would want to bet your life?

Notes

An Invitation to Come Inside

1. Evelyn Waugh, "Come Inside," in *The Essays, Articles, and Reviews of Evelyn Waugh,* ed. Donat Gallagher (Boston: Little, Brown, 1983), p. 368.
2. Scriptural citations are from the Revised Standard Version of the Bible. Psalms are quoted from the Grail Psalter.

1. Is Jesus the Only Savior?

1. Richard John Neuhaus, "To Say Jesus Is Lord," *First Things* 107 (November 2000), p. 69.
2. *Pastoral Constitution on the Church in the Modern World,* 22.

3. John Paul II, *Dives in Misericordia* [Rich in Mercy], 7.
4. John Paul II, *Letter Concerning Pilgrimage to the Places Linked to the History of Salvation,* 10.
5. John Paul II, *Dives in Misericordia,* 7.
6. John Paul II, *Redemptor Hominis* [The Redeemer of Man], 10.
7. See *Catechism of the Catholic Church,* 357.
8. Cited in ibid., 460.
9. Ibid.
10. St. Augustine, *Confessions* I:1.
11. See *Catechism of the Catholic Church,* 377.
12. *Pastoral Constitution on the Church in the Modern World,* 24.
13. See Robert W. Jenson, "How the World Lost Its Story," *First Things* 36 (October 1993), pp. 19–24.
14. See John Paul II, *Redemptor Hominis,* 1.
15. See *Pastoral Constitution on the Church in the Modern World,* 1.
16. Hans Urs von Balthasar, *Credo: Meditations on the Apostles' Creed* (New York: Crossroad, 1990), pp. 53–54.
17. See Rodney Stark, *The Rise of Christianity: How the Obscure, Marginal Jesus Movement Became the Dominant Religious Force in the Western World in a Few Centuries* (New York: HarperCollins, 1997). Stark is particularly insistent that "Christian women enjoyed substantially higher status within the Christian subcultures than pagan women did in the world at large" (p. 128).
18. John Paul II, *Redemptor Hominis,* 4.
19. See John Paul II, *Redemptoris Missio* [The Mission of the Redeemer], 29.

20. Hans Urs von Balthasar, *In the Fullness of Faith: On the Centrality of the Distinctively Catholic* (San Francisco: Ignatius Press, 1988), p. 20.
21. See George Weigel, *Witness to Hope: The Biography of Pope John Paul II* (New York: HarperCollins, 1999), p. 864.

2. Does Belief in God Demean Us?

1. See Henri de Lubac, S.J., *The Drama of Atheistic Humanism* (San Francisco: Ignatius Press, 1995).
2. Franz Werfel, *The Song of Bernadette* (New York: St. Martin's Press, 1970), pp. 259–60.
3. Peter Kreeft offers "An Extremely Brief Summary of 24 Arguments for God's Existence" in *Summa of the Summa: The Essential Philosophical Passages of St. Thomas Aquinas'* Summa Theologica *Edited and Explained for Beginners* (San Francisco: Ignatius Press, 1990), pp. 63–64.
4. *Catechism of the Catholic Church,* 31.
5. Peter L. Berger, *A Rumor of Angels: Modern Society and the Rediscovery of the Supernatural* (Garden City, N.Y.: Doubleday Anchor Books, 1970), pp. 53–75.
6. John Paul II, *Dives in Misericordia,* 4.
7. Ibid., 5–6.
8. *Catechism of the Catholic Church,* 237.
9. This brief exposition of the doctrine of the Trinity is adapted from Hans Urs von Balthasar, *You Crown the Year with Your Goodness: Sermons Throughout the Liturgi-*

cal Year (San Francisco: Ignatius Press, 1989), pp. 141–45.

10. See Hans Urs von Balthasar, *In the Fullness of Faith,* p. 111.

3. Liberal Church? Conservative Church?

1. *Dogmatic Constitution on the Church,* 6.
2. See John Paul II, "The Mission of the Church," in *Springtime of Evangelization,* ed. Thomas D. Williams, L. C. (San Diego: Basilica Press, 1999), pp. 45–52.
3. See *Dogmatic Constitution on the Church,* 3.
4. See John Paul II, "The Mission of the Church," in *Springtime of Evangelization.*
5. See Avery Dulles, S. J., *Models of the Church* (Garden City, N.Y.: Doubleday, 1974), and "Imaging the Church for the 1980s," in *A Church to Believe In* (New York: Crossroad, 1982), pp. 1–18.
6. See John Paul II, "The Mission of the Church," in *Springtime of Evangelization.*
7. See *Dogmatic Constitution on the Church,* 31. On the priestly mission of all the baptized, see ibid., 10; on the prophetic mission, see *Constitution on the Sacred Liturgy,* 12; on the royal mission of service, see *Dogmatic Constitution on the Church,* 36.
8. See *Dogmatic Constitution on the Church,* chapter 5.
9. See John Paul II, "Annual Address to the Roman Curia," in *L'Osservatore Romano,* English Weekly Edition, January 11, 1988, pp. 6–8.

10. On these points, see Hans Urs von Balthasar, *In the Fullness of Faith,* pp. 55–57.
11. See Hans Urs von Balthasar, *Theo-Drama IV: The Action* (San Francisco: Ignatius Press, 1994), pp. 92–93.

4. Where Do We Find the "Real World"?

1. *Catechism of the Catholic Church,* 1069.
2. See ibid., 1070.
3. Evelyn Waugh, *Men at Arms,* in *The Sword of Honour Trilogy* (London: Penguin Books, 1984), p. 61.
4. *Constitution on the Sacred Liturgy,* 14.
5. Ibid.
6. Joseph Cardinal Ratzinger, *The Spirit of the Liturgy* (San Francisco: Ignatius Press, 2000), pp. 22–23.
7. M. Francis Mannion, "The Success of Liturgical Reform," *Antiphon: A Journal of Liturgical Renewal* 5, no. 2 (2000), p. 2.
8. *Constitution on the Sacred Liturgy,* 8.
9. John Paul II, "Gift of the Priesthood," in *Springtime of Evangelization,* p. 78.
10. On these issues, see Benedict M. Ashley, O. P., *Justice in the Church: Gender and Participation* (Washington, D.C.: Catholic University of America Press, 1996).
11. *Catechism of the Catholic Church,* 2560.
12. Evelyn Waugh, *Unconditional Surrender,* in *The Sword of Honour Trilogy,* p. 438.
13. See *Catechism of the Catholic Church,* 2562–63.

5. How Should We Live?

1. Servais Pinckaers, O.P., *The Sources of Christian Ethics* (Washington, D.C.: Catholic University of America Press, 1995), p. 164.
2. *Catechism of the Catholic Church,* 1719.
3. Ibid., 1723.
4. See Pinckaers, *The Sources of Christian Ethics,* pp. 355–56.
5. See ibid., pp. 367–72.
6. Cited in *L'Osservatore Romano*, English Weekly Edition, March 1, 2000, pp. 1–2 [emphases in original].
7. John Paul II, General Audience Address, March 1, 2000, in *L'Osservatore Romano,* English Weekly Edition, March 8, 2000, p. 11.
8. *Catechism of the Catholic Church,* 387.
9. See John Paul II, *Dominum et Vivificantem* [Lord and Giver of Life], 38.
10. G.K. Chesterton, *Orthodoxy* (Garden City, N.Y.: Doubleday Image Books, 1959), p. 121.
11. Robert Bolt, preface to *A Man for All Seasons* (New York: Vintage Books, 1962), pp. xiii, xi.
12. Bolt, *A Man for All Seasons,* pp. 76–77.
13. See *L'Osservatore Romano,* English Weekly Edition, November 8, 2000, p. 3.
14. John Paul II, *Veritatis Splendor,* 58.
15. Bolt, *A Man for All Seasons,* p. 81.
16. Bolt, preface to *A Man for All Seasons,* pp. xi–xii.
17. "Retiring Cardinal's Legacy Broadens Reach of Church," *Washington Post,* December 25, 2000, p. A14.
18. On these points, see Gilbert Meilaender, "The First

of Institutions," *Pro Ecclesia* 6, no. 4 (fall 1997), pp. 44ff.

6. How Should We Love?

1. Karol Wojtyła, *Love and Responsibility* (San Francisco: Ignatius Press, 1993).
2. See Rocco Buttiglione, *Karol Wojtyła: The Thought of the Man Who Became Pope John Paul II* (Grand Rapids: Eerdmans, 1997), pp. 90–91.
3. John Paul II, *Original Unity of Man and Woman* (Boston: St. Paul Books and Media, 1981), p. 73.
4. Ibid, pp. 73–74.
5. John Paul II, *Blessed Are the Pure of Heart* (Boston: St. Paul Books and Media, 1983), p. 185.
6. Ibid., p. 229.
7. Ibid., pp. 241–46.
8. John Paul II, *The Theology of Marriage and Celibacy* (Boston: St. Paul Books and Media, 1986), p. 40.
9. Ibid., pp. 215–24.
10. Ibid., pp. 363–68.
11. John Paul II, *Reflections on* Humanae Vitae (Boston: St. Paul Books and Media, 1984), pp. 35–40.
12. Ibid.
13. Elizabeth Wirth, "Like a Natural Woman," *Regeneration Quarterly* 6, no. 4 (winter 2000), p. 27.
14. Pontifical Council for the Family, *Vademecum for Confessors Concerning Some Aspects of the Morality of Conjugal Life*, 11.

15. *Code of Canon Law,* 980.
16. John Paul II, *The Theology of Marriage and Celibacy,* pp. 215–24.
17. *Catechism of the Catholic Church,* 1629.
18. Joseph Cardinal Ratzinger, *Salt of the Earth: The Church at the End of the Millennium* (San Francisco: Ignatius Press, 1997), p. 207.
19. *Catechism of the Catholic Church,* 2357.
20. Ibid., 2358.

7. Why Do We Suffer?

1. John Paul II, *Salvifici Doloris,* 2.
2. Ibid., 5.
3. Ibid., 2.
4. Ibid., 7.
5. Ibid., 12.
6. Ibid., 13.
7. Ibid., 18.
8. Ibid.
9. Hans Urs von Balthasar, *Credo: Meditations on the Apostles' Creed* (New York: Crossroad, 1990), p. 52.
10. Hans Urs von Balthasar, *The Threefold Garland* (San Francisco: Ignatius Press, 1982), pp. 99, 101.
11. John Paul II, *Salvifici Doloris,* 14.
12. Ibid., 19.
13. Ibid.
14. Ibid., 20.
15. See ibid., 22.

16. Ibid., 23.
17. See ibid.
18. Ibid., 23–24.
19. Ibid., 26.
20. Ibid., 27.
21. Ibid., 29.
22. Ibid., 30.
23. Ibid., 27.
24. Ibid., 31.
25. *Pastoral Constitution on the Church in the Modern World,* 22.
26. Peter Kreeft, *Making Sense out of Suffering* (Ann Arbor, Mich.: Servant Books, 1986), p. 184.

8. What About the Rest of the World?

1. See *Dogmatic Constitution on the Church,* 8.
2. John Paul II, *Ut Unum Sint* [That May Be One], 1, 9.
3. See *John* 17.20–21.
4. See John Paul II, *Ut Unum Sint,* 54, 57. John Paul II returned to this point, in an even sharper way, in his apostolic letter closing the Great Jubilee of 2000: "By fixing our gaze on Christ, the Great Jubilee has given us a more vivid sense of the Church as a mystery of unity. 'I believe in the one Church': what we profess in the Creed *has its ultimate foundation in Christ,* in whom the Church is undivided (cf. *1 Corinthians* 1.11–13). As his Body, in the unity which is the gift of the Spirit, she is indivisible. The reality of division among the Church's children

appears at the level of history, as the result of human weakness in the way we accept the gift which flows endlessly from Christ the Head to his Mystical Body" (*Novo Millennio Ineunte* [At the Beginning of the New Millennium], 48, emphasis in original).

5. See John Paul II, *Ut Unum Sint,* 48, 83.
6. *Dogmatic Constitution on the Church,* 8. An ocean of ink has been spilled over the meaning of "subsists" in Vatican II's description of the relationship between the one Church of Christ and the Catholic Church. That the Council fathers intended to move beyond the claim that the one Church of Christ is identical with the Catholic Church is clear from the history of the drafting of the *Dogmatic Constitution on the Church,* during which the Latin phrase *subsistit in* [subsists in] was substituted for the claim that the one Church of Christ "is" the Catholic Church, period. My formulation of the meaning of "subsists in" is borrowed from Father Richard John Neuhaus.
7. *Dogmatic Constitution on the Church,* 8.
8. See ibid.
9. *Decree on Ecumenism,* 3.
10. This is what the controversial declaration *Dominus Iesus* meant when it said that for the sake of theological accuracy, the term "Church" should be used of some Christian communities but not of others (*Dominus Iesus,* 17). The declaration went on to repeat the teaching of Vatican II that all the baptized "are incorporated in Christ and thus are in a certain communion, albeit imperfect, with the Catholic Church."
11. John Paul II, *Ut Unum Sint,* 21.

12. Ibid., 88, 95, 96.
13. See John Paul II, "Address in the Synagogue of Rome," in *Spiritual Journey: Texts on Jews and Judaism 1979–1995,* ed. Eugene J. Fisher and Leon Klenicki (New York: Crossroad, 1995), p. 63.
14. For the full text of "Speak the Truth," see *First Things* 107 (November 2000), pp. 39–41.
15. Joseph Cardinal Ratzinger, *Many Religions—One Covenant: Israel, the Church and the World* (San Francisco: Ignatius Press, 1999), pp. 103–4.
16. Cited in Dennis R. Hoover, "Rome, Relativism, and Reaction," *Religion in the News* 3, no. 3 (fall 2000), p. 14.
17. John Paul II, *Redemptoris Missio,* 9, 10 [emphasis in original].
18. See Congregation for the Doctrine of the Faith, *Dominus Iesus,* 21–22.
19. John Paul II, *Redemptoris Missio,* 62.
20. Ibid., 2.
21. Ibid., 46.
22. Ibid., 50.
23. Ibid., 4.
24. Ibid., 39 [emphasis in original].
25. John Paul II, "Address to the Fiftieth General Assembly of the United Nations Organization," 9.

9. Is Catholicism Safe for Democracy?

1. Robert Suro, "Pope, on Latin Trip, Attacks Pinochet Regime," *New York Times,* April 1, 1987, pp. A1, A10.

2. John Paul II, *Centesimus Annus,* 46.
3. John Paul II, *Veritatis Splendor,* 96.
4. Ibid., 97.
5. John Paul II, *Evangelium Vitae* [The Gospel of Life], 57.
6. Some have argued that the unborn child in an unwanted pregnancy, particularly in the case of rape, is an "aggressor" and is thus not an "innocent" human being: abortion, on this proposal, is thus a legitimate act of self-defense by the mother. To this, John Paul II responds that "no one more absolutely innocent could be imagined." A defenseless unborn child, even in the tragic circumstances of rape, remains an innocent with an inalienable right to life (see ibid., 58).
7. John Paul II, "Address to Ambassador Corinne Boggs," *L'Osservatore Romano*, English Weekly Edition, December 31, 1997, p. 4.
8. *Catechism of the Catholic Church,* 2278, 2279. The *Catechism* also teaches that "the use of painkillers to alleviate the sufferings of the dying, even at the risk of shortening their lives, can be morally in conformity with human dignity if death is not willed as either an end or a means, but only foreseen and tolerated as inevitable" (2279).

10. What Will Become of Us?

1. Aldous Huxley, *Brave New World* (New York: Bantam Modern Classics, 1968), pp. 119–20.
2. Waugh to John Betjeman, November 9, 1950, in *The*

Letters of Evelyn Waugh, ed. Mark Amory (New York: Penguin Books, 1982), pp. 339–40.

3. See Robert Royal, *The Catholic Martyrs of the Twentieth Century: A Comprehensive World History* (New York: Crossroad, 2000). At the "Commemoration of the Witnesses to the Faith in the Twentieth Century" held in the Roman Coliseum on May 7, 2000, John Paul II made sure that Orthodox and Protestant martyrs were recognized with their Catholic brethren.
4. See the glossary of the *Catechism of the Catholic Church.*
5. John Paul II, *Novo Millennio Ineunte,* 30, 31.

Acknowledgments

My first word of thanks must go to my editor and friend, Diane Reverand, who first proposed this kind of book and then did a fine job of counseling me on both its substance and its accidents, as an older generation of Catholics might have said.

Loretta Barrett, Ever Horan, Father Jay Scott Newman, and Joan Weigel made important comments on the manuscript. Father Thomas Williams, L.C., provided crucial logistical help in Rome, and Rosemary Horan tracked down a stray Chestertonism. I am also grateful for the continuing support, in friendship and prayer, of the priests and people of St. Jane Frances de Chantal Parish in Bethesda, Maryland.

Some of the ideas here were first explored in my weekly column in the Catholic press; my best thanks to Kay Lagreid, of the *Catholic Northwest Progress* in Seattle, and to her colleagues for inviting me to write the column and for seeing to its syndication. I have also borrowed a few ideas from commencement addresses I gave in 2000 at Sacred Heart Major Seminary in Detroit, St. Mary's Seminary and University in Baltimore, St. Vincent Seminary in Latrobe, Pennsylvania, and the University of Dallas. I am grateful to those fine institutions for their gifts of honorary degrees and for inviting me to think through some of the most basic issues of Catholic life in the twenty-first century.

G. W.
19 March 2001
Solemnity of Joseph, Husband of Mary